Easy Traditional Quilting

by

Lora Rocke

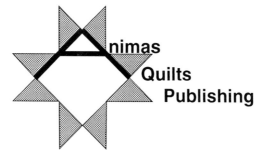
Animas Quilts Publishing

600 Main Ave.
Durango, CO. 81301
(970) 247-2582

Easy Traditional Quilting

Animas Quilts Publishing
600 Main Ave.
Durango, CO. 81301
(970) 247-2582

ISBN: 1-885156-15-4

Printed on Recycled Paper

CREDITS:	
Editor	Kim Gjere
Graphics	Lora Rocke
	Jackie Robinson
Photography	Christopher Marona

Printed in Colorado

MEET LORA ROCKE

Growing up on the plains of Nebraska, Lora learned a love of art and needlework from her maternal grandmother. "Grammy taught me a little bit of everything, but mostly she showed me how to improvise with color, design, and materials." In 197 she completed her first quilt from pieces begun by her great-grandmother. Since then, over 100 projects have been completed, a majority of them machine quilted. Lora enjoys being able to produce a traditional art form quickly. Creating something both practical and beautiful is the best of both worlds.

Lora lives with her husband and daughter in Lincoln, Nebraska where she creates, teaches, lectures, writes and quilts.

DEDICATION

With love for Joe.

ACKNOWLEDGEMENTS

This book was made possible by a husband who trusts me, a daughter who hugs me, and parents who love me. It was also pushed and prodded along by quilting friends who lent their support and were never afraid to offer advice, suggestions and encouragement. Lastly, this is my quiet way of acknowledging those strong women who have quilted before me with imagination and ingenuity.

TRODUCTION

In 1829 a marvelous, magical machine was eated. By the 1840s it could sew faster, straighter d produce stronger stitches than any woman. If it as within her means, a woman purchased and ized this wonderful tool. Most of the quilts from e 1800s and early 1900s are pieced and quilted hand. But the reason they were may lie not in a oman's choice of technique, but in her affluence. If e had the chance I think she would have chosen e quickest way to create warmth and protection for r family, especially for the utility quilts. Granted, e sewing machines of those days couldn't come ar to creating the quality or beauty of hand uilting. But today's machines can.

Ten years ago I began machine quilting. I love the ok of lots of quilting, but I don't love the process of nd quilting. And I admit, I am not the best quilter ound. Harriet Hargrave's book "Heirloom Machine uilting" inspired me and I was supported by other uilters who were trying to machine quilt. After sev- al aborted attempts when either the tension was f, the thread broke, the batting was wrong or the hole thing slipped away from me, I produced a uilt. I realized almost any quilting design could be ne if I practiced and took my time.

Trying to achieve a traditional look was my goal. ke most quilters, I looked to the past for inspira- on. I searched out antique quilting designs and dapted them to my projects. I would play with the es, finding that with slight changes, it could ecome a continuous line design without losing the d fashioned feel. The wonderful side benefit of ese designs is that they help my hand quilting go ster too! Many of the motifs in this book will elimi- te the need for the hand quilter to start and stop often.

Included here are the fruits of long wonderful urs spent looking at quilts. The quilts of the 800s and early 1900s were the focus of my search. Several sources are listed in the bibliogra- y. I looked at photographs, slides, books, and agazines. I went to gallery exhibits, museum and uilt show exhibits, auctions, flea markets, and ntique shops. I visited with people. I was in eaven. I hope that you are able to use this book to art machine quilting slowly and relatively stress e. With practice and patience you will be able to ove on to larger and more challenging designs. Remember: Tools may change, but Art is con- ant.

CONTENTS

BIBLIOGRAPHY/INSPIRATION

Houck, Carter, and Myron Miller. American Quilts and How to Make Them. Charles Scribner's Sons, 1975.

Nelson, Cyril I., and Carter Houck. Treasury of American Quilts. Greenwich House/Arlington House, Inc., 1982.

Orlofsky, P., and M. Orlofsky. Quilts in America. McGraw-Hill Book Co., 1974.

Pellman, Rachel, and Kenneth Pellman. The World of Amish Quilts. Good Books, 1984.

Quilts

Sheldon Memorial Art Gallery Quilt Exhibit for Nebraska Quilts and Quiltmakers

Nebraska State Historical Society Quilt Exhibits

Quilts by Fern Godfrey, Minnie Godfrey, and unknown women.

Quilts at antique shops, flea markets, bazaars, and auctions.

Other Suggested Reading

Cleland, Lee. Quilting Makes the Quilt. Bothell, WA: That Patchwork Place, 1994.

Fanning, Robbie, and Tony Fanning. The Complete Book of Machine Quilting, 2d ed. Radnor, PA: Chilton Book Co., 1994.

Hargrave, Harriet. Heirloom Machine Quilting, rev. ed. Lafayette, CA: C & T Publishing, 1995.

Johanna, Barbara. Continuous Curve Quilting. Menlo Park, CA: Pride of the Forest, 1980.

Noble, Maurine. Machine Quilting Made Easy. Bothell, WA: That Patchwork Place, 1994.

SUPPLIES

Needles

Always start a new project with a new needle. There may be invisible burrs or a blunt end on the needle that you have been using. Good sizes for machine quilting are #70/10 or #80/12. A #60/8 can be used with nylon thread.

Threads

I recommend a good quality cotton thread (50/3). For the bobbin use either regular weight or machine quilting thread. Invisible or smoke nylon thread is also available at your local quilt shop. The combinations of top thread and bobbin thread depend on you and your sewing machine. You can quilt with regular thread on top and in the bobbin, regular thread/quilting thread, regular/nylon, quilting/quilting, nylon/nylon, nylon/regular. Try out the combination before you begin to quilt your project. Practice with fabric, thread, and batting that are the same as those used in the project. Soon you will find combinations that both you and your sewing machine like.

Walking Foot

This foot is designed to move the top fabric along at the same speed as the bottom fabric. The walking foot may be used for quilting straight lines, diagonals or gentle curves. It is a great tool for beginners, but it does have drawbacks. When quilting sharp angles or squares, you will need to turn the whole project.

Darning Foot

This foot is used for free motion techniques. The feed dogs on most machines must be dropped to use the darning foot. I use this foot for virtually all my quilting. It is especially useful for doodling, feathering, and sharp angles and turns. You will usually be able to reverse direction without turning the quilt.

Batting

A large variety of battings are now on the market. Each gives a different look and feel to a quilted piece. I prefer to use a cotton batting or a high-content cotton batting. They are easy to handle and require slightly less basting because they don't shift easily. Cotton batting is also flatter than polyester batting, more comfortable, and easy to quilt with the sewing machine.

The main reason I like cotton batting is that once is washed the batting shrinks, giving the quilt added dimension and an old fashioned look. This will help non-traditional quilting techniques look more traditional. If you are just beginning to machine quilt, it can help to hide less than perfect stitches. To minimize the shrinkage, prewash or presoak cotton batting according to manufacturer's directions. Quilting requirements differ from batting to batting. Check the package; it will include suggested quilting distances. Remember, too, that quilting "eats up" some of the length and width of the quilt. Allow about 2" around the edges to accommodate for this.

GENERAL DIRECTIONS

Block Size

All of the designs in this book are sized for an 8" block (finished) or a 4" border (finished). If you need a different size please feel free to use a copy machine to enlarge or reduce the design. Since it is time consuming to guess about the percentages to be used, the following chart may be helpful. Most copy machines are limited in their reduction or enlargement percentages. You may have to do a little addition and more than one copy to achieve the correct size.

For example, you wish to change a 4" border to a 6" border. Starting at the 4" column, move down to the 6" line. You will need to enlarge the design 150%. If you are changing to a size not on the chart, like 5-1/2", use the percentage halfway between 5" (125%) and 6" (150%) or 137%.

	4"	8"
1"	25%	12%
2"	50%	25%
3"	75%	37%
4"	100%	50%
5"	125%	62%
6"	**150%**	75%
7"	175%	87%
8"	200%	100%
9"	225%	112%
10"	250%	125%
11"	275%	137%
12"	300%	150%

Transferring the Design

There are several ways to transfer the designs to the quilt top. First photocopy the design you wish to use to the correct size. Use one of the following methods to mark the quilt top.

1. Use a light box. You may use a homemade device or a commercially made light box. Tape the copied design on the glass. Place the quilt top over the copy. Mark the quilt top by tracing the design onto the top with a mechanical pencil, pencil or marker of your choice.

2. Create a stencil. Trace and cut a stencil onto cardstock or heavy mylar using the copied design. Remember to leave "bridges" between cutouts or the whole thing will fall apart. More intricate designs may prove difficult. Mark the quilt top with the pencil or marker of your choice.

3. Use bridal netting as a tracing medium. Cut a piece of netting or tulle, slightly larger than the copied design. Don't use too fine a mesh or you will be unable to trace the pattern onto the quilt top. Lay netting over the copy and trace the design with a permanent waterproof marker. Let the marker dry for a minute or two. Pin the netting in place on the quilt top. Trace over the design on the netting using pencil, chalk or marker.

4. Free hand draw. Once the copy is to size, often you can use a plate, dish or saucer as a template. This works especially well for the swags and vines. (After all, our grandmothers probably did it that way.)

5. Con-tact® Self Adhesive Plastic. Trace shapes or templates onto the plastic. Peel away backing and stick the template to the quilt top. Quilt around the shape(s) then peel off and reposition in another place. Cut several templates at one time. When the sticky stuff is gone, stick on a new template and begin again. No marking is necessary.

6. Spray the back of a photocopied quilting design with 3-M Spray Mount™ Artist's Adhesive. Stick it to the quilt top and machine quilt right through the paper. Tear away the paper pattern, pulling slightly on the quilt surface. It leaves no residue.

7. Use a quilting guide that attaches to the walking foot to quilt straight or diagonal rows.

Centering the Border Design

The border design creates a frame for the inner quilt. These designs can repeat the central design; relate to, but be different from the central design; or be a continuation of the central design. Unpieced borders consist of two parts. The strips and the corners. The strips are along the sides, top, and bottom of the quilt. The corners can be visualized as a square in each corner of the quilt.

Borders can be quilted in a couple of ways. Repetition of a single design (hearts, figure eights, flowers) or continuous designs (vines and swags). The design can be continuous and round the corner:

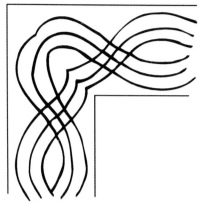

It can run off the edges:

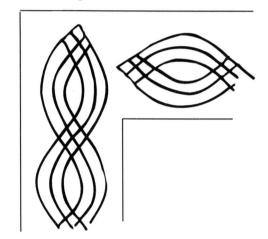

Or it can break completely and have something different in the corner:

Running the design off the ends of the quilt is the easiest form of border design. Next is the different corner, then the rounding of the corner. Some possible corner treatments are given with the border designs. You may have other ideas, try them!

To mark the design and plan its placement, first find the middle of each side of the quilt. Center the design unit on that point. Transfer the design to the border. Extend or contract the design slightly, if needed. It should run off the edge of the quilt or end at the imaginary square in the corner in preparation for the turn or an alternate design. Then use either the corner treatment illustrated or place a different motif in the corner. Repeat the process for the remaining corners.

Quilt Sandwich

Preparing the three layers for quilting is probably the most important step in the entire process. If you get sloppy, the end product may not be as you expect. Start out small and work your way up to a larger project.

1. Cut the backing fabric 2" - 4" larger than the quilt top. Mark the center point. Press and lay it flat, wrong side up on a table. Use binder clips, about every foot, to secure the backing to the edge of the table. For smaller quilts, clip two sides to the edges of the table and tape the other sides to the table.

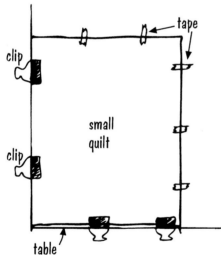

For quilts larger than the table, spread backing taut and clip. Then work with one half of the quilt at a time, matching centers and working outward.

2. Lay the batting on top of the backing, matching center points and smoothing out all of the wrinkles. Remove binder clips one at a time and replace to include the batting.

3. Place the center of the quilt top in the center of the batting/backing. Smooth out the quilt top and re-clip the sides one clip at a time. The quilt sandwich should be wrinkle free and taut, but not distorted or larger than the backing fabric.

4. Baste all layers together. You may use the traditional method of needle and thread making long running stitches. This is a good method for smaller projects but not the best for larger quilts that will be handled a lot. You may want to pin baste by using 1" rustproof safety pins. Pin through all layers about every 3" - 4". Be sure not to place pins where you will be quilting. Cotton batting requires less pins since it shifts less than polyester batting. You will need approximately 250-300 pins for a full sized quilt. Whichever way you baste, begin at the center and work out vertically, horizontally, and diagonally.

5. Begin quilting once the sandwich is complete. at all possible, quilt vertical, horizontal, or diagonal rows first to anchor the three layers. Start at the to center and quilt through the sashings and borders out to the sides.

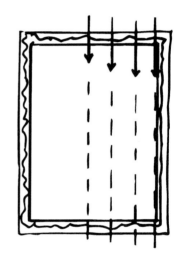

Or begin at the center of a side and quilt horizontal through the quilt.

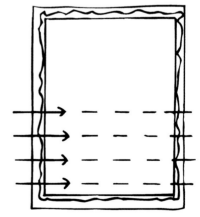

Or start at an upper corner and follow a diagonal

...e through the center of the quilt.

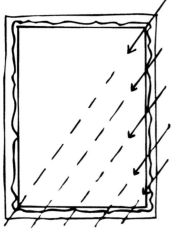

Always start at the center line and quilt in the same direction to the outer edges. Turn the quilt and repeat the process on the other side. If there re no long lines to follow, start with the center lock, quilt it, then move out from the center in horizontal or diagonal rows.

After the anchoring rows have been quilted, begin the center and quilt the designs on the blocks and ashings. Work from the center outward. Quilt the orders last. Begin in the center of the border if ossible or with a stabilizing curve or spine.

ome Things to Consider

Practice! Trust me—it does get easier. Like any ther art form, the more you practice, the better it ooks and the more comfortable you'll feel.

Smaller projects are more easily manipulated nder the sewing machine. The process of quilting ny design is the same, but in a larger quilt, you annot twist and turn the piece as easily, if at all. he most difficult designs to produce are circular or ose that come back on themselves, and believe it r not, straight lines or stitch-in-the-ditch.

Practice the main design once or twice before eginning, following the arrows, on paper or on fabc. Sometimes it is enough practice transferring the esign repeatedly onto the quilt top. Any practice ill help you get the rhythm of the design.

Look ahead and anticipate your direction. You on't always be able to see exactly where the line is oing.

A solid color fabric shows off quilting stitches best. onversely, if you wish to be more discreet in your uilting, use a print or a busy floral (especially as e backing).

Many of the quilts from the 1800s used two lines f stitching when one would suffice. Not just outline itching but double stems, curves, circles, vines,

etc. You can achieve an "older" look by quilting two rows instead of one.

Typically, the fill-in or background would come up to the pieced block but would not continue through the design. This didn't apply if the entire top was quilted in an overall pattern.

Try to see past the basic outline of a pieced block. Begin to think in other terms. What design would complement the block? What would enhance or emphasize it? If the quilt is basically curved pieces, think straight line quilting and vice versa.

Remember to lift your foot off the foot feed before you sneeze!

THE DESIGNS

Each chapter is organized from easiest to most difficult. The difficulty level is indicated at the bottom of each design page by one, two, or three sewing machine needles. One is the easiest, three the most difficult.

Each design is dated. Some of these are approximations.

Always begin quilting a design at the star and follow the arrows. Complete directions are given with each design.

Straight Lines and Braids

This is a good beginning chapter. Start these designs using the walking foot. As you feel more confident move on to using a combination of walking foot and darning foot where appropriate. In some designs either foot will work. My preference is listed first. The darning foot will be used often.

Feathers and Ferns

This chapter features designs which contain very traditional feather, fern and leaf motifs. With most of these designs it will be helpful to quilt a baseline curve first. This will help to stabilize the quilt sandwich. If you follow the arrows and the directions you will be able to quilt an entire design unit without breaking off the thread.

Hearts and Flowers

Emphasizing the use of hearts or flowers, many of the smaller motifs may be used with designs from other chapters.

Seasonal and Swag

All of the seasons and some holidays are represented in this chapter. The swags are fun and can be used with other single motifs from the other chapters. I have given several alternate placement ideas for use in borders and full sized blocks.

Straight Lines
and Braids

CROSS HATCH
< parallel >

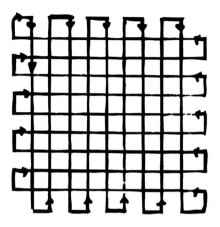

CROSS HATCH
< random - parallel >

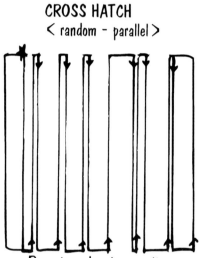

Repeat random in opposite
direction to achieve a plaid.
Stitch-in-the-ditch around
block to finish.

CROSS HATCH
< diagonal - even >

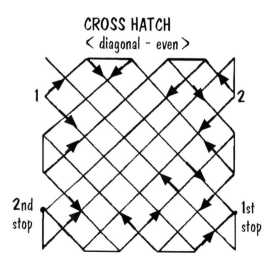

DOODLE

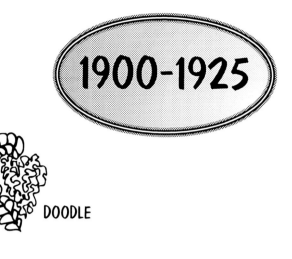

ECHO

CORNER OR BORDER TREATMENT

CROSS HATCH
< diagonal - double line >

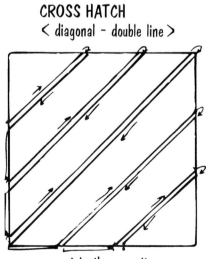

- repeat in the opposite
  direction for more fill
- increase angle for a
  diamond effect

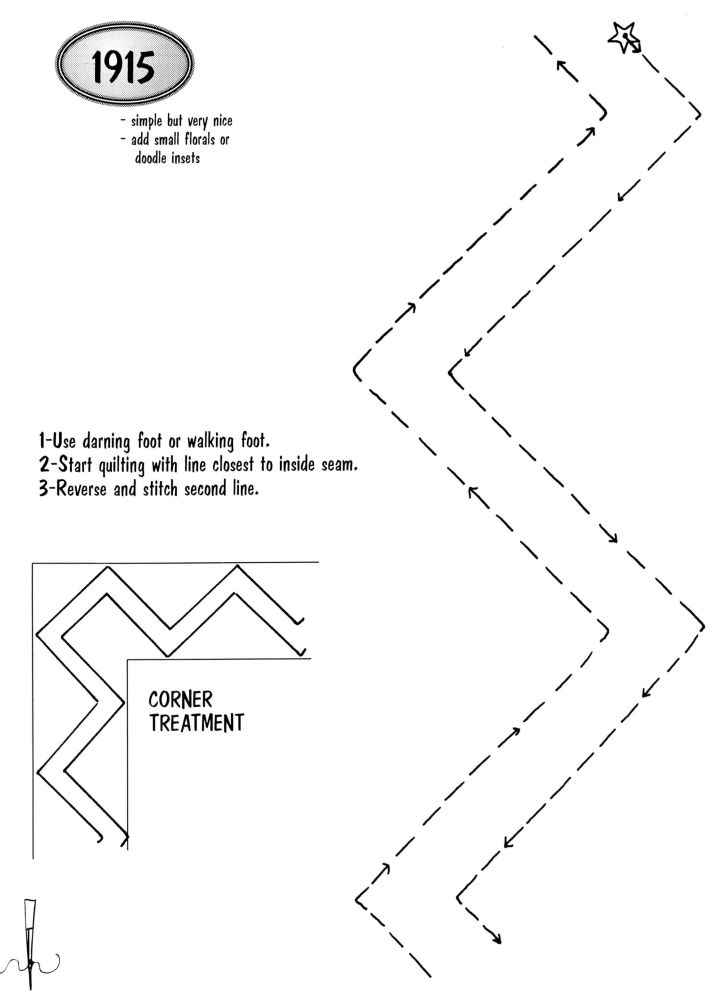

1915

- simple but very nice
- add small florals or
  doodle insets

1-Use darning foot or walking foot.
2-Start quilting with line closest to inside seam.
3-Reverse and stitch second line.

CORNER
TREATMENT

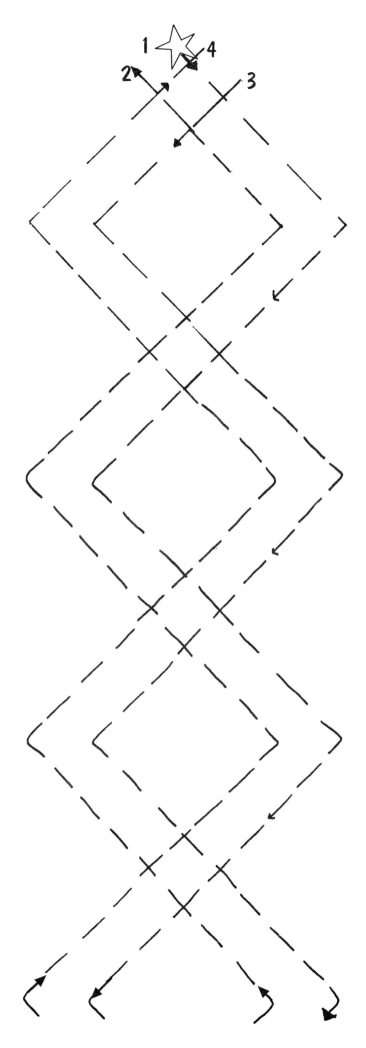

-simple braid

1-Use darning foot or walking foot.
2-Starting at inside seam, quilt the first line to the end. Quilt over to second line and quilt back to the beginning.
3-Repeat with rows 3 and 4.

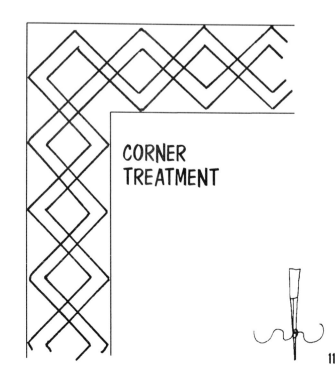

CORNER
TREATMENT

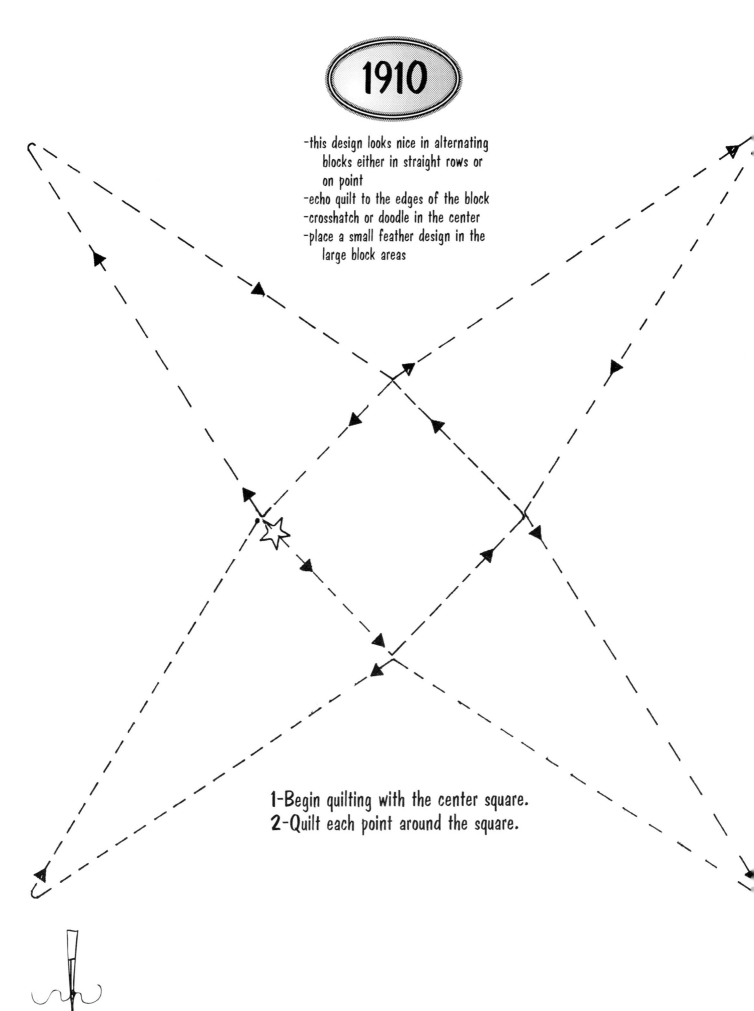

1910

-this design looks nice in alternating
  blocks either in straight rows or
  on point
-echo quilt to the edges of the block
-crosshatch or doodle in the center
-place a small feather design in the
  large block areas

1-Begin quilting with the center square.
2-Quilt each point around the square.

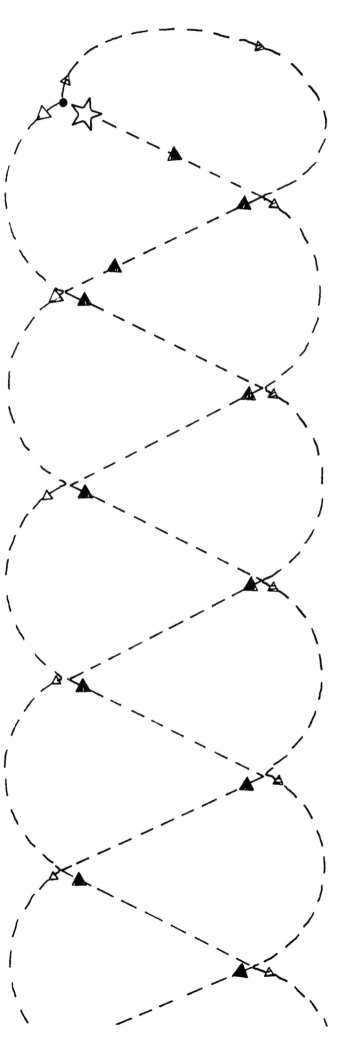

1-Sew zig-zag down the center of border or sash. Use darning foot or walking foot.
2-With darning foot quilt scallop along left side.
3-Quilt scallop along end and right side.

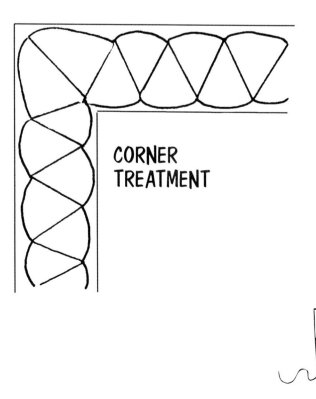

CORNER TREATMENT

1905

1-Use darning foot or walking foot.
2-Start at seamline of border. Begin with inside
   row and quilt to the outside edge. Quilt line
   1 down entire length of border or sashing.
3-Reverse direction and echo line **2**. Repeat
   with line **3**.
4-Repeat process on the opposite side of the
   braid.

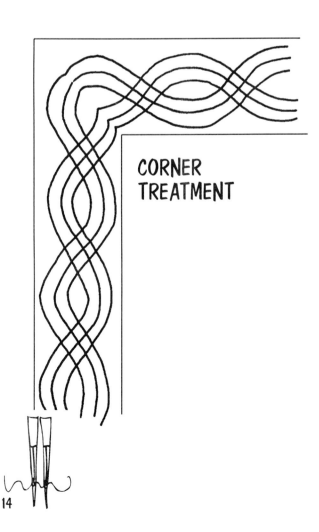

CORNER
TREATMENT

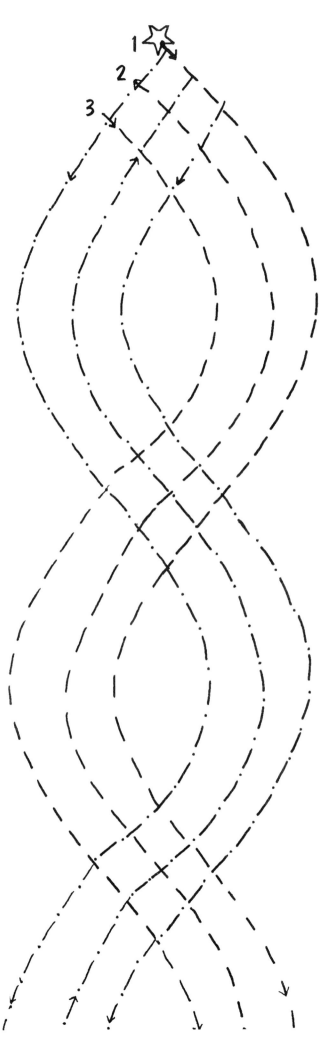

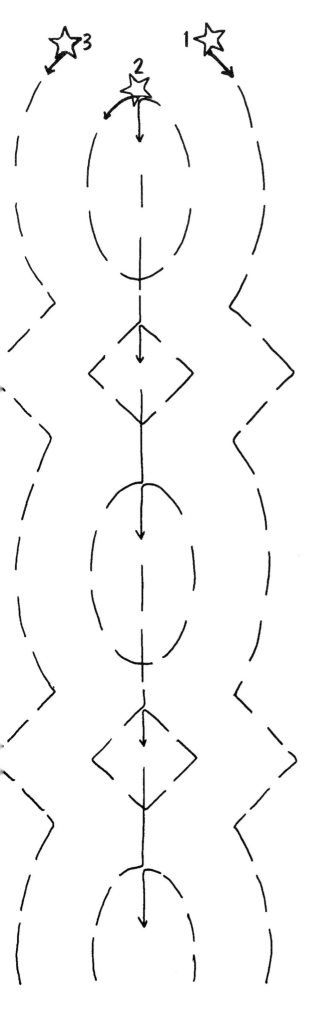

1-Use darning foot.
2-Quilt line **1** < closest to seam >.
3-Quilt center motif, line **2**, following
    arrows.
4-Quilt outer edge, line **3**.

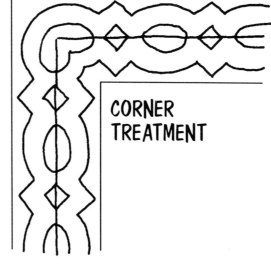

CORNER
TREATMENT

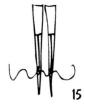

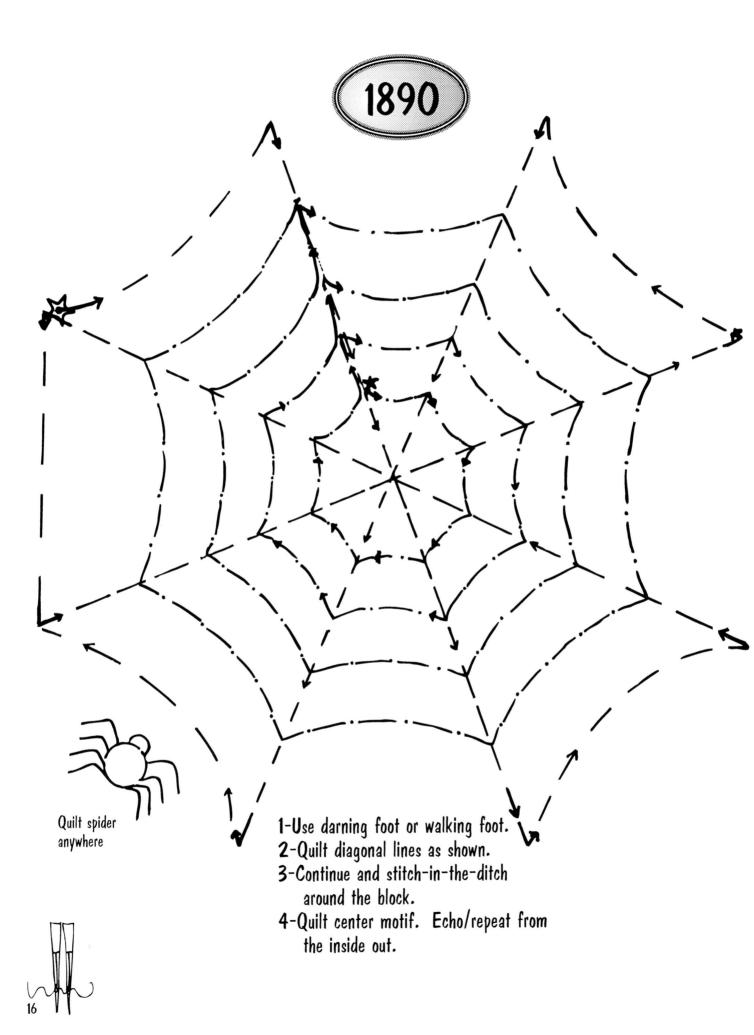

1890

Quilt spider
anywhere

1-Use darning foot or walking foot.
2-Quilt diagonal lines as shown.
3-Continue and stitch-in-the-ditch
   around the block.
4-Quilt center motif. Echo/repeat from
   the inside out.

16

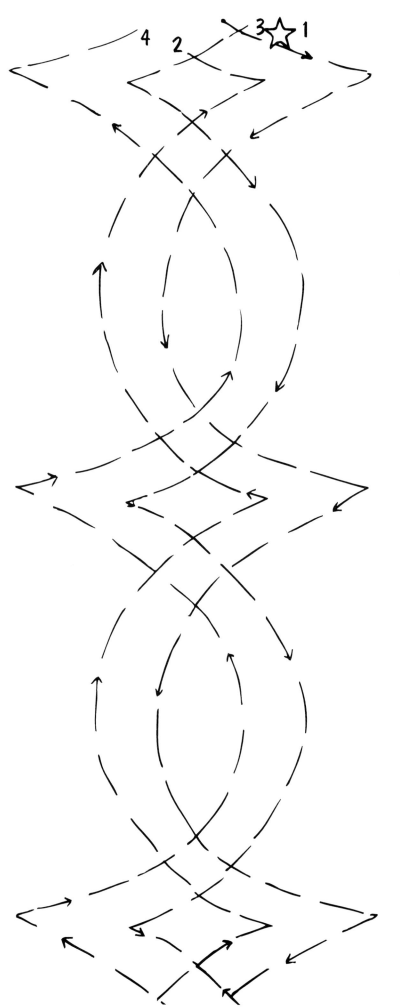

1-With darning foot and starting at inside
 seam line, quilt line **1** to the end. Stitch
 over to line **2** and quilt back to the
 beginning.

2-Quilt line **3**. Stitch over to the 4th line
 and quilt back to the beginning.

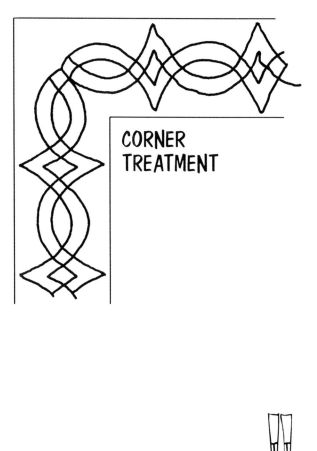

CORNER
TREATMENT

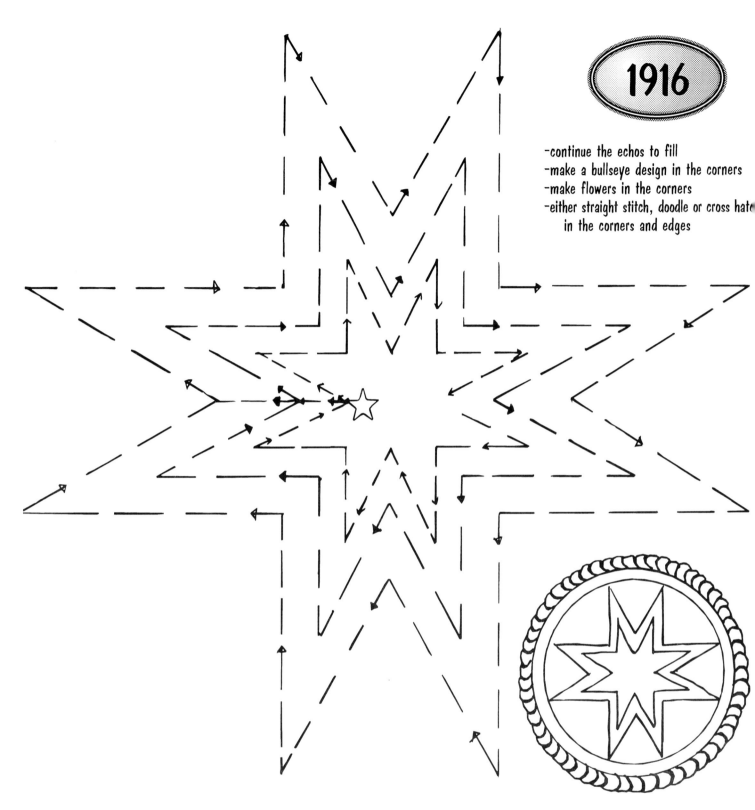

- continue the echos to fill
- make a bullseye design in the corners
- make flowers in the corners
- either straight stitch, doodle or cross hatc(
   in the corners and edges

1-Use darning or walking foot. Darning foot is easier, no
   turning of project.
2-Begin with the center star.
3-Travel to the next star and echo stitch outward.

Example of combination wreath/star.
Wreath from page 34 without
inside feathers.

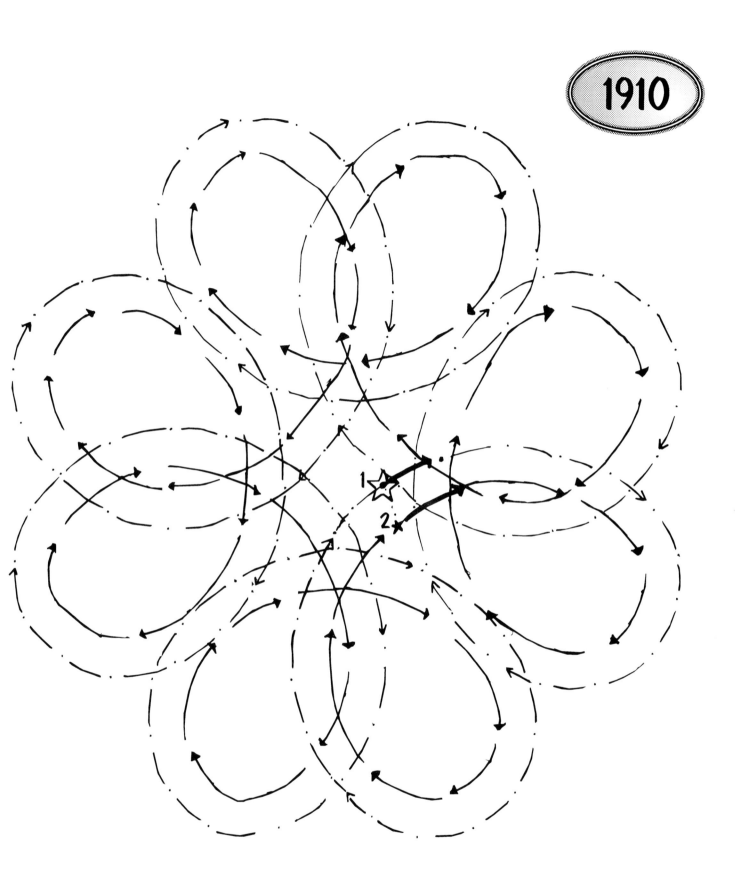

1-Use darning foot.

2-Start at star 1. Pretzel loop around creating the outside edges of the design.

3-Reposition needle and echo 1st quilting lines to form the inside edges.

1-Use darning foot or walking foot.

2-Start at seamline side of border; quilt line **1**. Reverse direction and quilt line **2** to the beginning. Do likewise with lines **3** and **4**.

3-Repeat with other set of quilting lines. Start at inner line and work toward outer edge.

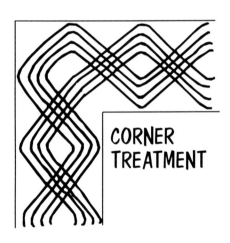

CORNER
TREATMENT

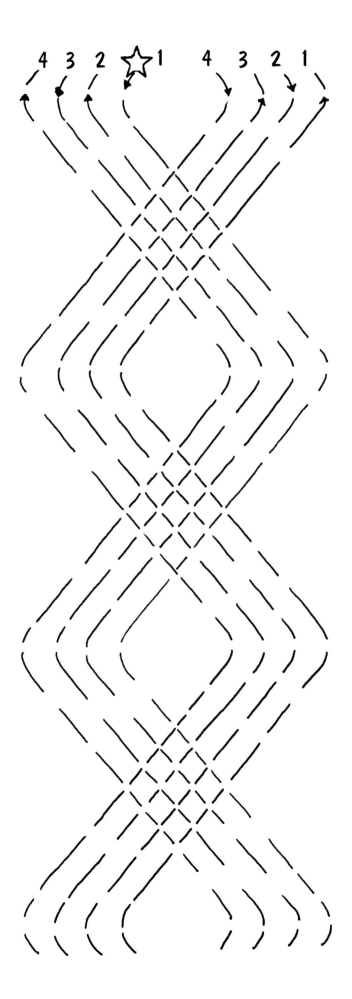

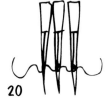

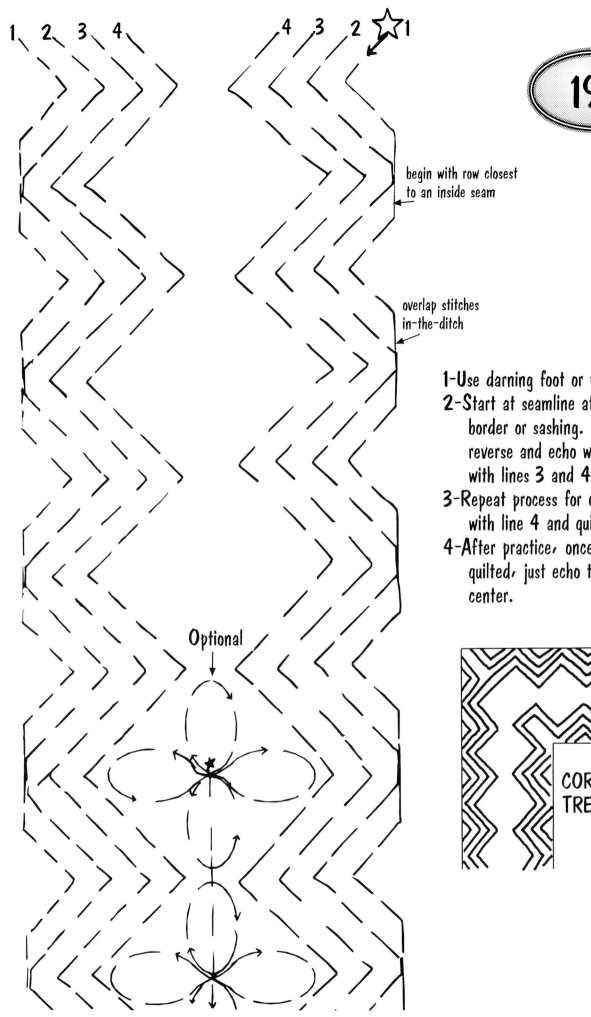

1   2   3   4   4   3   2   ☆ 1

begin with row closest
to an inside seam

overlap stitches
in-the-ditch

1-Use darning foot or walking foot.
2-Start at seamline at inside of the
   border or sashing. Quilt line 1,
   reverse and echo with line 2. Repeat
   with lines 3 and 4. Break thread.
3-Repeat process for other side starting
   with line 4 and quilting out to edge.
4-After practice, once the 1st row is
   quilted, just echo the lines to the
   center.

Optional

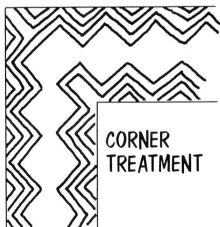

CORNER
TREATMENT

1918

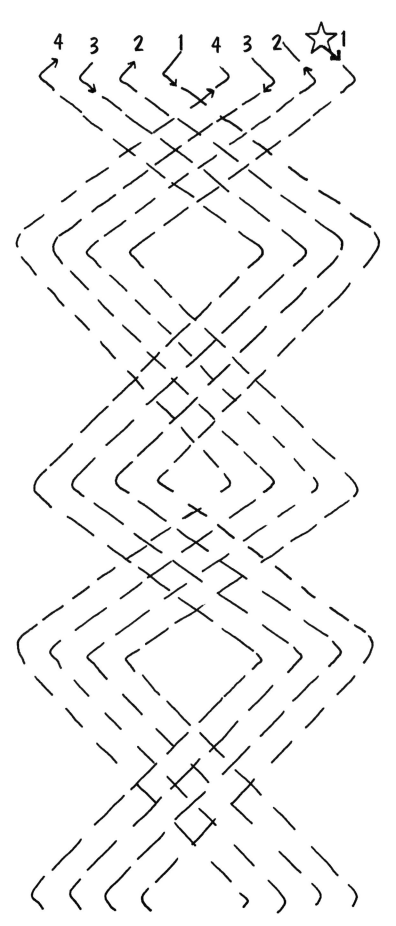

1-Use darning foot or walking foot.
2-Quilt line 1 closest to the inside seam line.
3-Reverse direction to quilt line 2.
4-Repeat with lines 3 and 4.
5-Repeat with the remaining set of quilting lines.

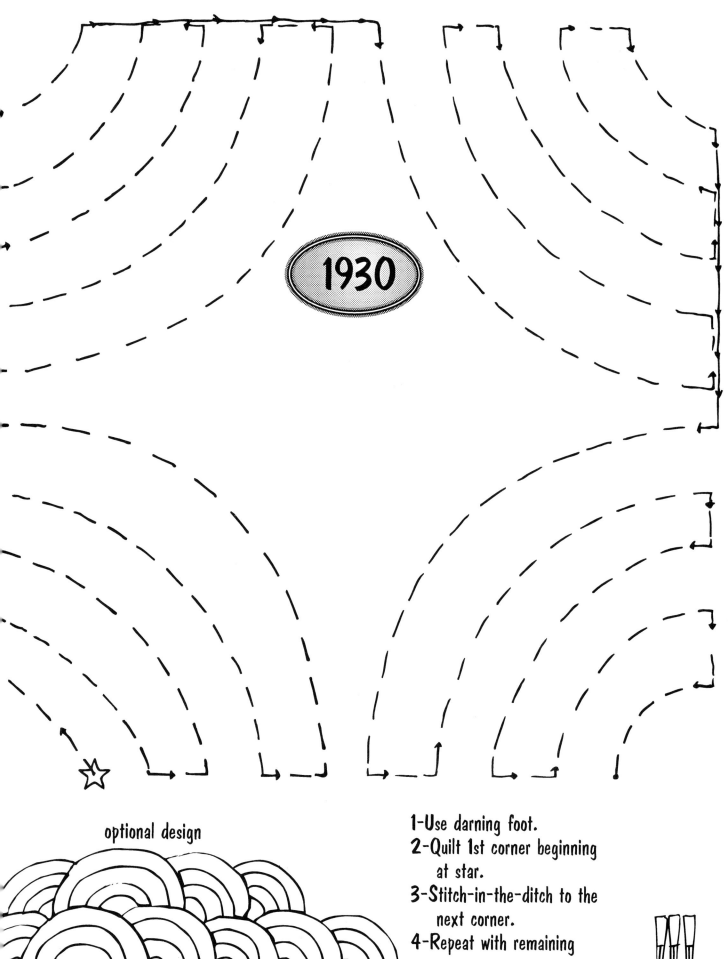

1930

optional design

1-Use darning foot.
2-Quilt 1st corner beginning at star.
3-Stitch-in-the-ditch to the next corner.
4-Repeat with remaining corners.

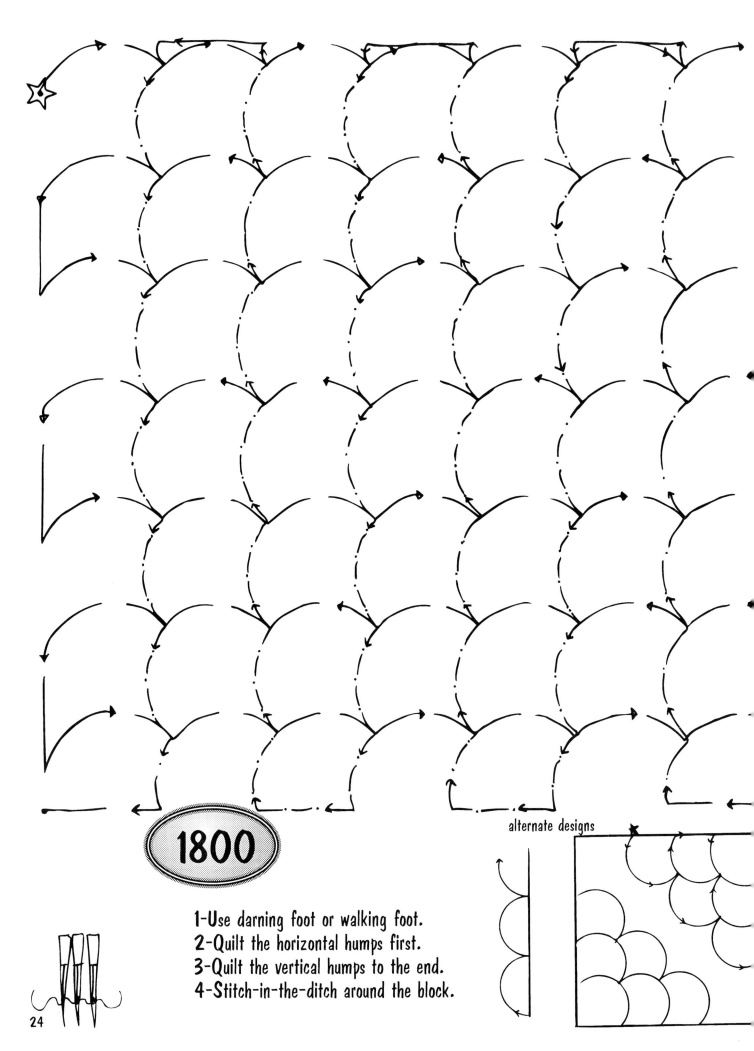

1800

1-Use darning foot or walking foot.
2-Quilt the horizontal humps first.
3-Quilt the vertical humps to the end.
4-Stitch-in-the-ditch around the block.

alternate designs

1-Use darning foot and begin at the star.
2-Quilt vertically from one side of block to the other side. Quilt the humps down the left side and back up.
3-Travel to next vertical row and quilt straight down.
4-Repeat to end.

1-Use darning foot.
2-Quilt horizontal rows first. Use quilting to move from row to row.
3-When horizontal rows are quilted travel in quilting design to the vertical rows.
4-When the last vertical row is completed finish quilting in pattern around the last two sides.

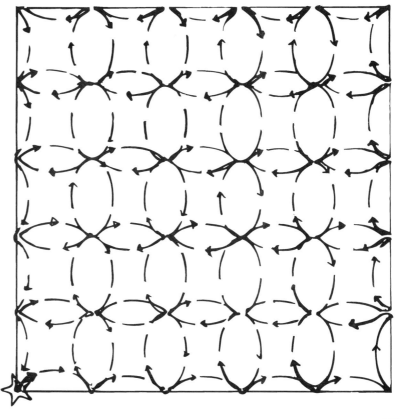

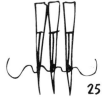

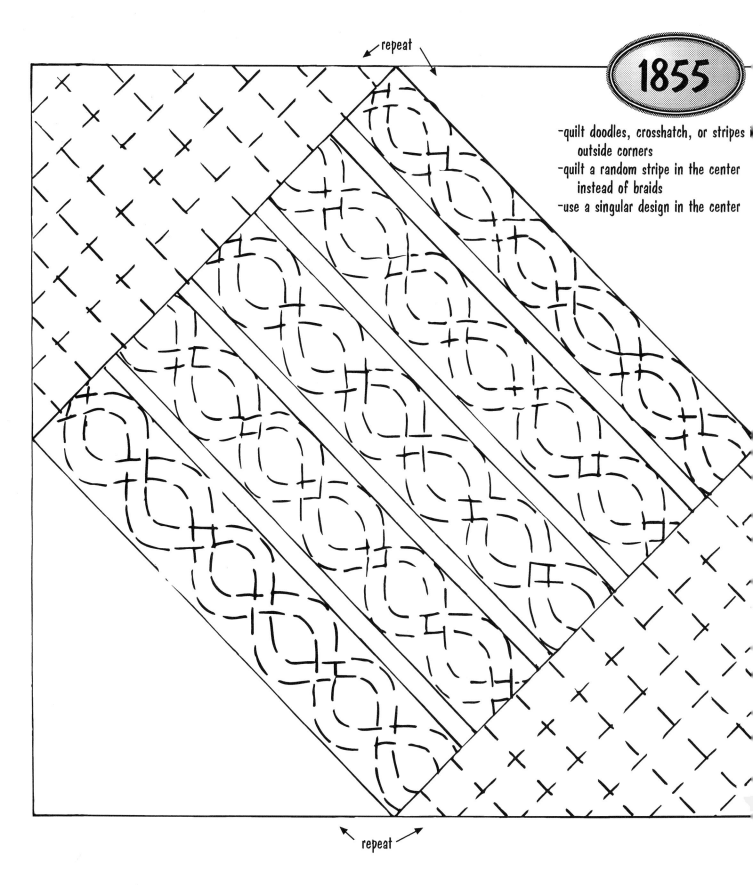

repeat

1855

- quilt doodles, crosshatch, or stripes outside corners
- quilt a random stripe in the center instead of braids
- use a singular design in the center

repeat

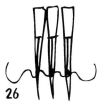

1-Use a darning foot.
2-There are several stops and starts.
3-Begin by quilting the inside square.
4-Then quilt the stripes, starting from the center.
5-Quilt the braids.
6-Quilt the outside corners last.

Feathers
and Ferns

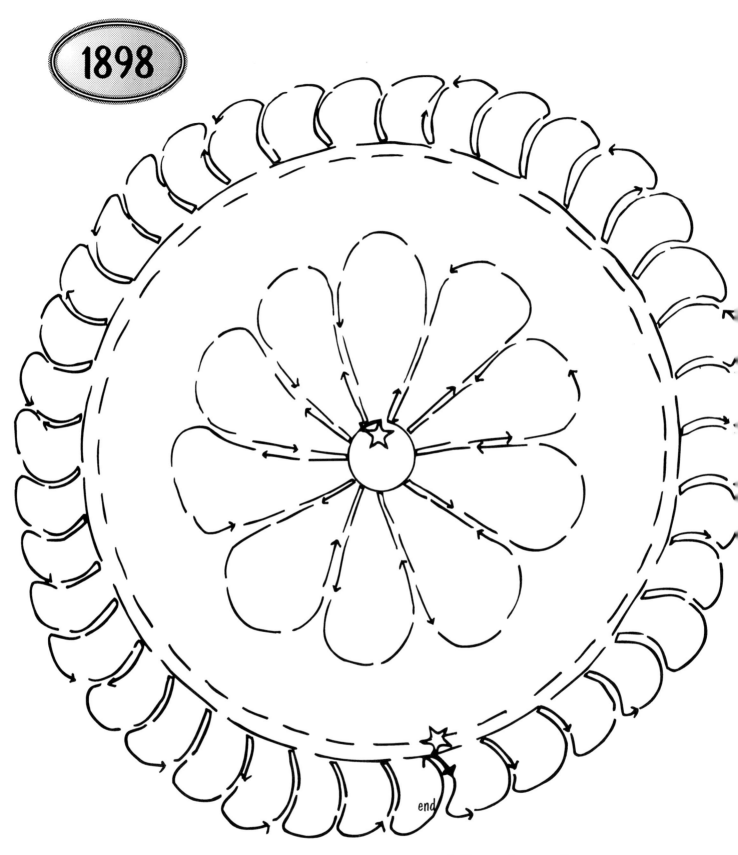

1898

end

1-Use a darning foot.
2-Sew circles first as a baseline.
3-Quilt inside design.
4-Then quilt outside ferns.

1898

-make one continuous vine or
join segments end to end
-add crosshatches or doodles in
empty spaces

1-Use the darning foot.
2-Quilt spine first.
3-Quilt one side of leaves.
4-Echo quilt the spine back to
   the beginning.
5-Quilt other side of leaves.

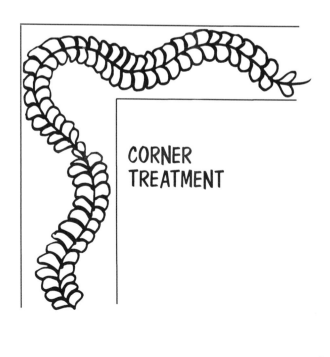

CORNER
TREATMENT

1-Use darning foot.
2-Quilt down right side of spine.
3-Quilt leaves on the right.
4-Quilt left spine, then left leaves.

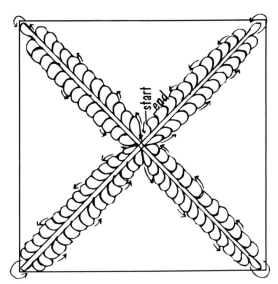

start end

FULL BLOCK TREATMENT
1-Sew diagonal lines first.
2-Begin at center and create ferns by stitching
    leaves first up one side of the diagonal then
    down the other side.
3-Repeat on all diagonals.

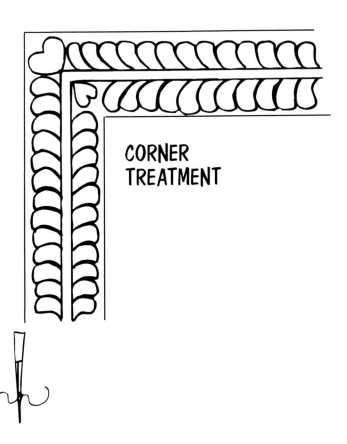

CORNER
TREATMENT

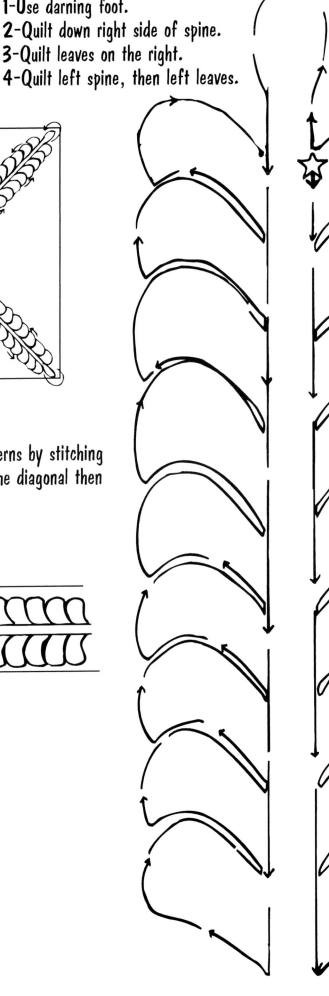

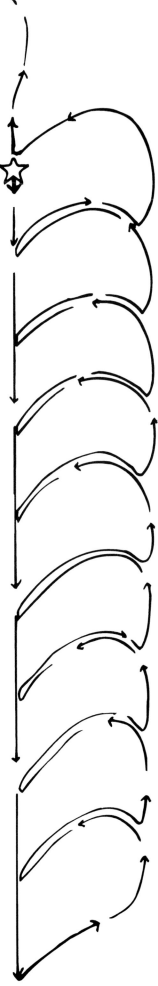

- doodle outside edges for an
  older look
- keep leaves rounded...think heart-shaped
- quilt spines as guides for leaves

1-Use darning foot.
2-Quilt small center circle first.
3-Quilt large outer circle.

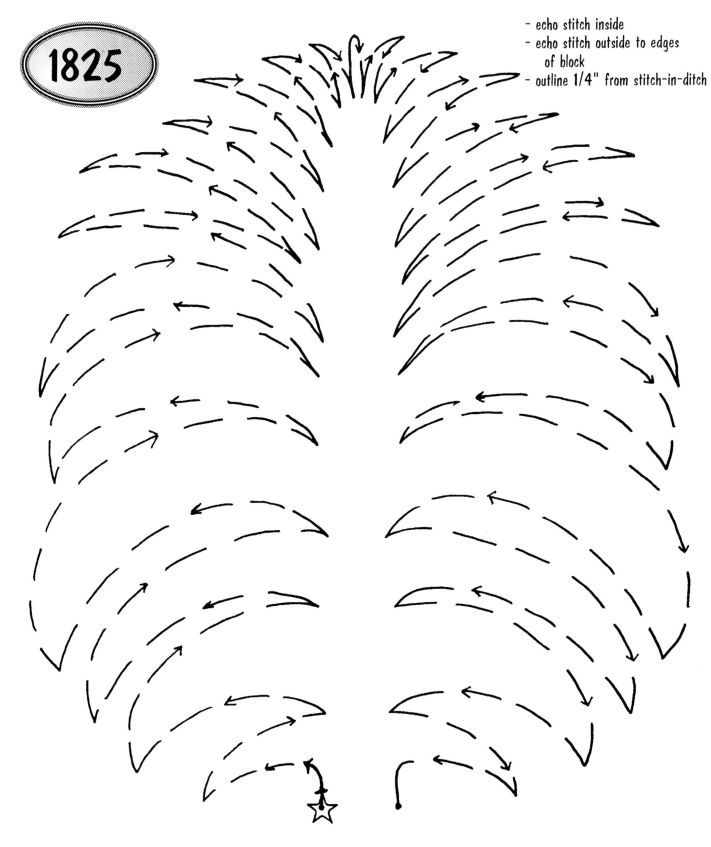

1825

- echo stitch inside
- echo stitch outside to edges of block
- outline 1/4" from stitch-in-ditch

1-Use darning foot.
2-Follow arrows.
3-Stitch-in-the-ditch when design is completed.

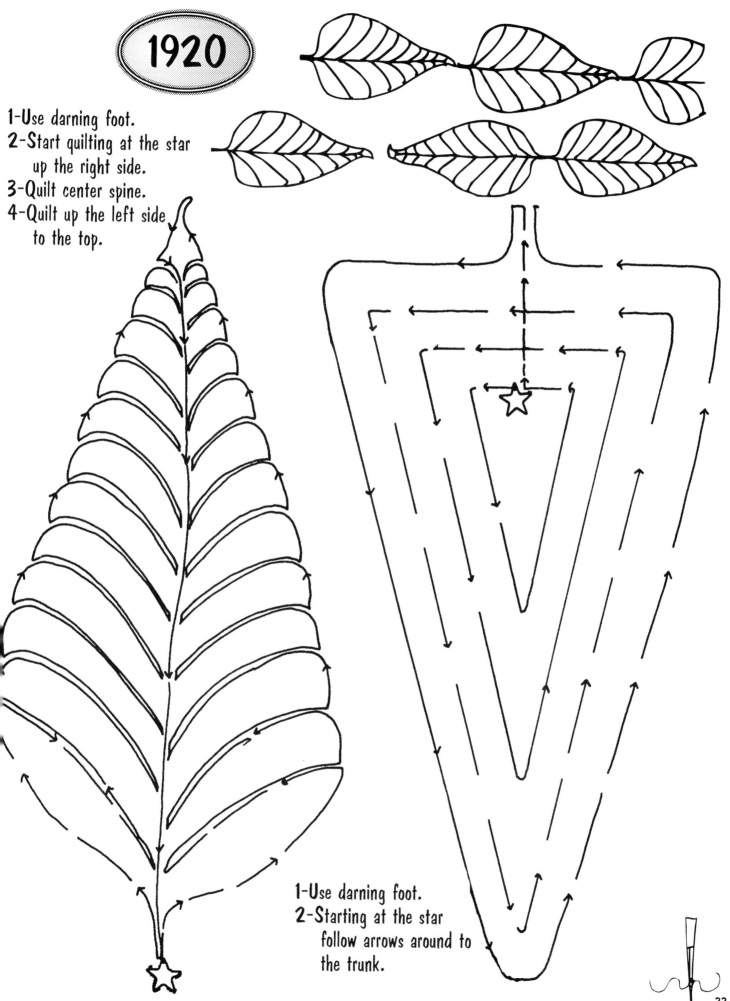

1920

1-Use darning foot.
2-Start quilting at the star
  up the right side.
3-Quilt center spine.
4-Quilt up the left side
  to the top.

1-Use darning foot.
2-Starting at the star
  follow arrows around to
  the trunk.

1851

- may be used with 1916 star on page 18

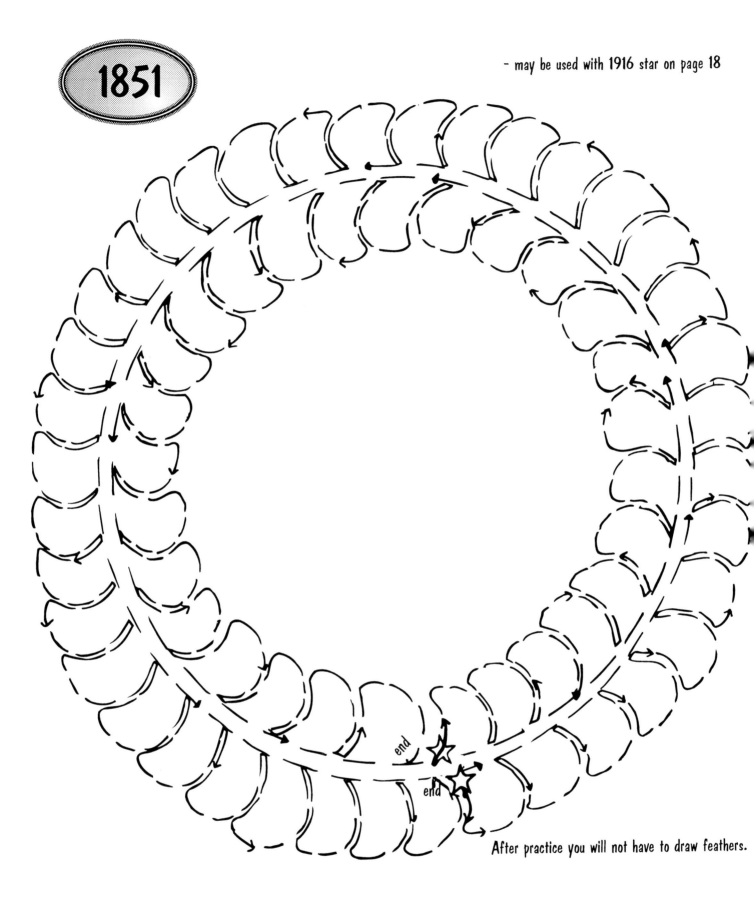

end

end

After practice you will not have to draw feathers.

1-Use darning foot.
2-Sew circles first.
3-Quilt feathers on the inside, then outside.

- crosshatch or doodle in center or outside edges
- eliminate inside leaves
- quilt name or initials in the center
- quilt single motif in the center
- quilt a smaller version of the heart in the center

1850

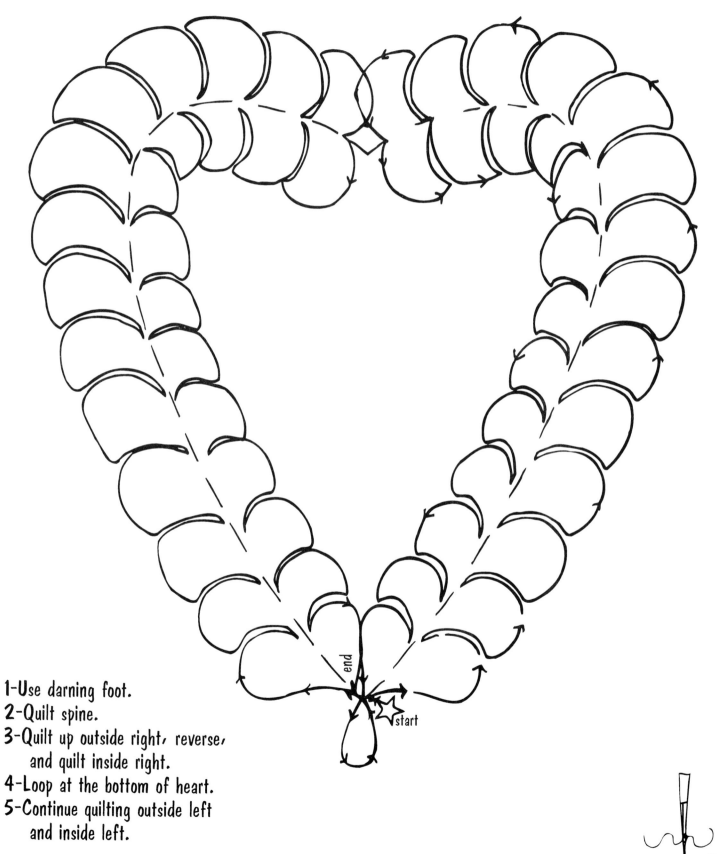

end

start

1-Use darning foot.
2-Quilt spine.
3-Quilt up outside right, reverse,
    and quilt inside right.
4-Loop at the bottom of heart.
5-Continue quilting outside left
    and inside left.

- doodle, stripe, crosshatch center or outside edges
- quilt a heart, feather or flower in the center
- echo quilt the outside edges

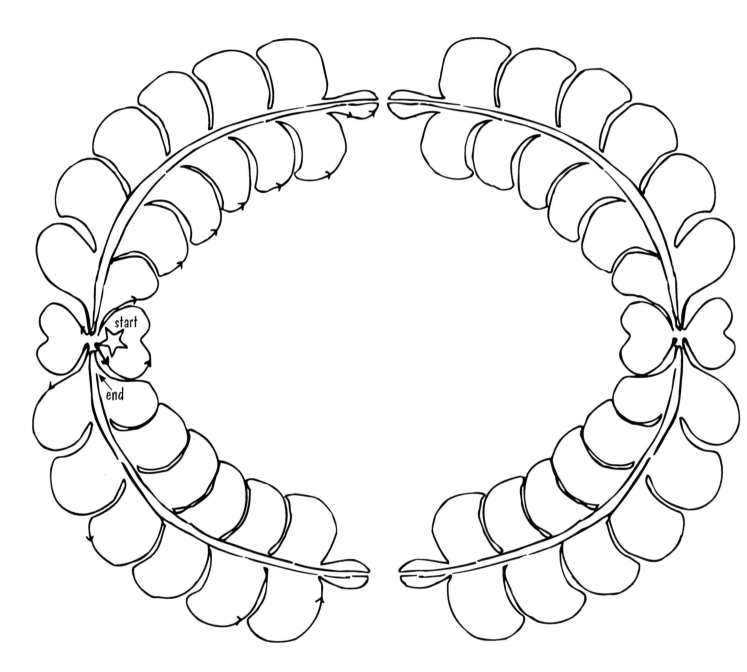

start

end

1-Use darning foot.
2-Quilt oval spine - one or two rows.
3-Begin quilting at an inside heart.
4-Quilt to the top-center of the oval.
5-Reverse directions and quilt down the outside until completing the heart.
6-Repeat process on the lower half and the opposite side.

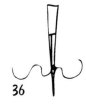

- crosshatch, stripe, doodle, or echo quilt the center
  and outside edges
- quilt a single motif in the center

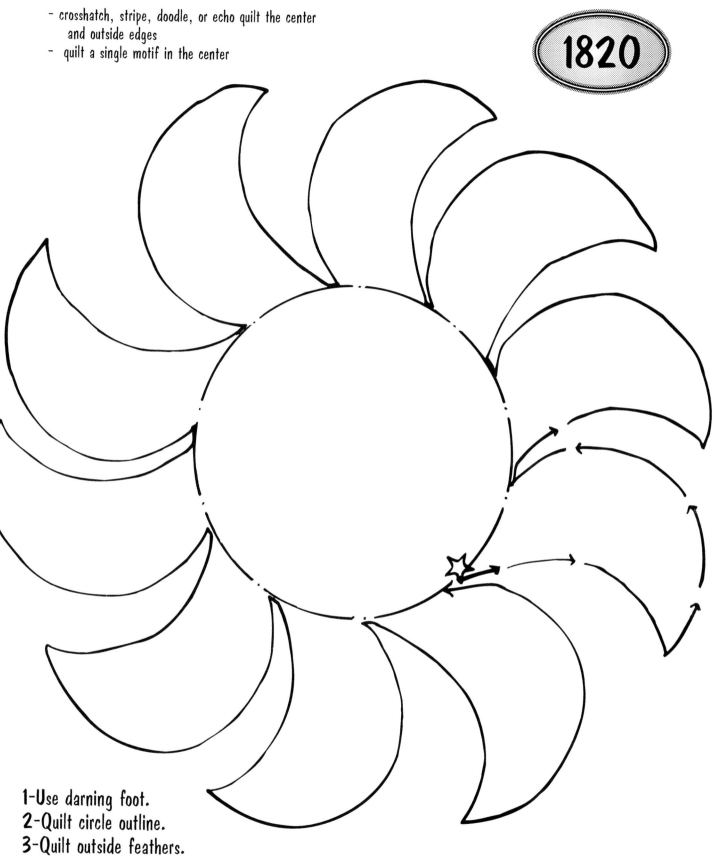

1-Use darning foot.
2-Quilt circle outline.
3-Quilt outside feathers.

1889

- crosshatch, doodle, or stripe in outer areas
- turn entire design on point

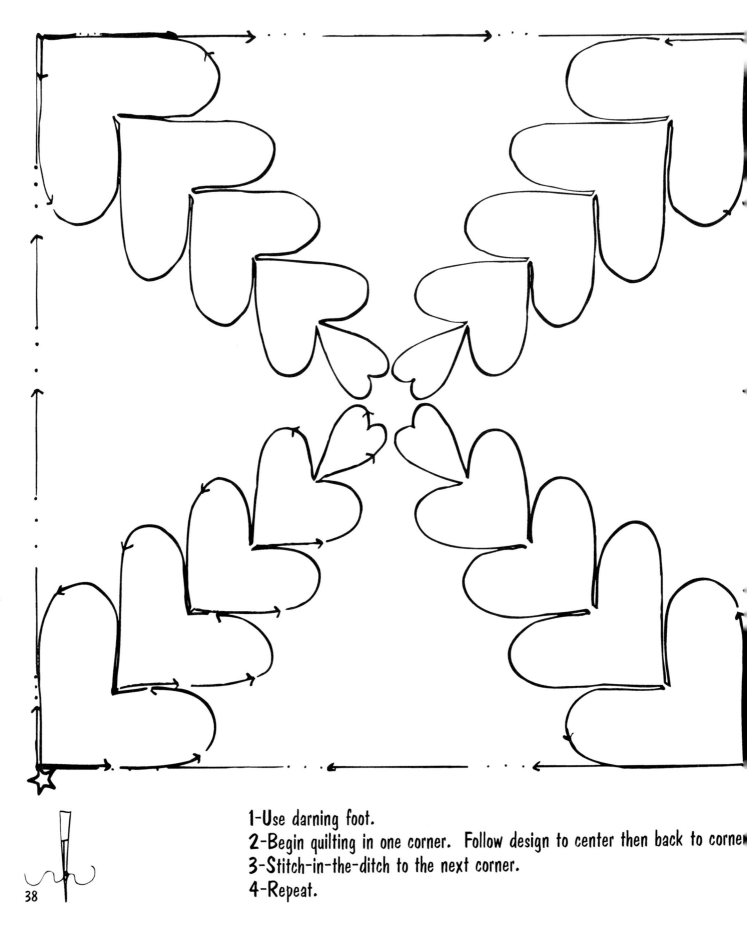

1-Use darning foot.
2-Begin quilting in one corner. Follow design to center then back to corner
3-Stitch-in-the-ditch to the next corner.
4-Repeat.

- echo stitch inside larger leaves
- omit inside leaves and crosshatch the center
- crosshatch, doodle, stripe or echo outside to block edges

1-Use darning foot.
2-Quilt center ivy leaves.
3-Quilt outside ivy.

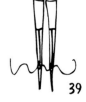

1829

– crosshatch center
– crosshatch, stripe or echo to outside edges

1-Use darning foot.
2-Quilt center loop-to-loop.
3-Quilt the feathers.

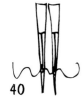

- use in combination with the **1825** leaves, page **32**, to create a
  pineapple in adjoining squares
- reduce these two designs to fit into a border
- eliminate crosshatching and quilt a name, initial, or single motif

1-**U**se darning foot.

2-**O**utline stitch double oval circles.

3-**C**rosshatch center...see page **9**.

4-**Q**uilt outside right leaves from bottom to the
   top circle.

5-**Q**uilt outside left from bottom to top.

1840

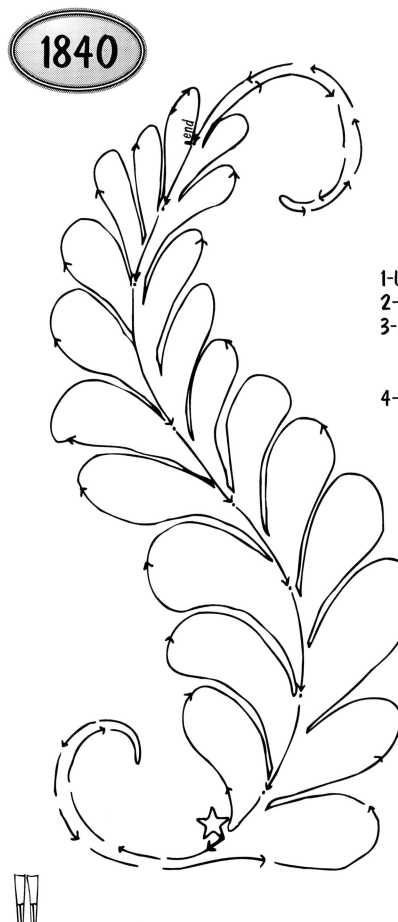

end

– crosshatch or doodle in the open areas

1–Use darning foot.
2–Start quilting at the star.
3–Proceed around the curl, up the right
    side, around the top curl, and down the
    center spine.
4–Quilt up the left side, ending at the top.

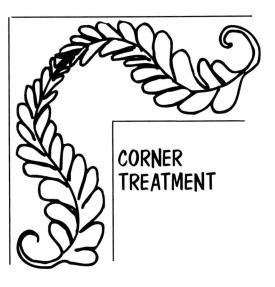

CORNER
TREATMENT

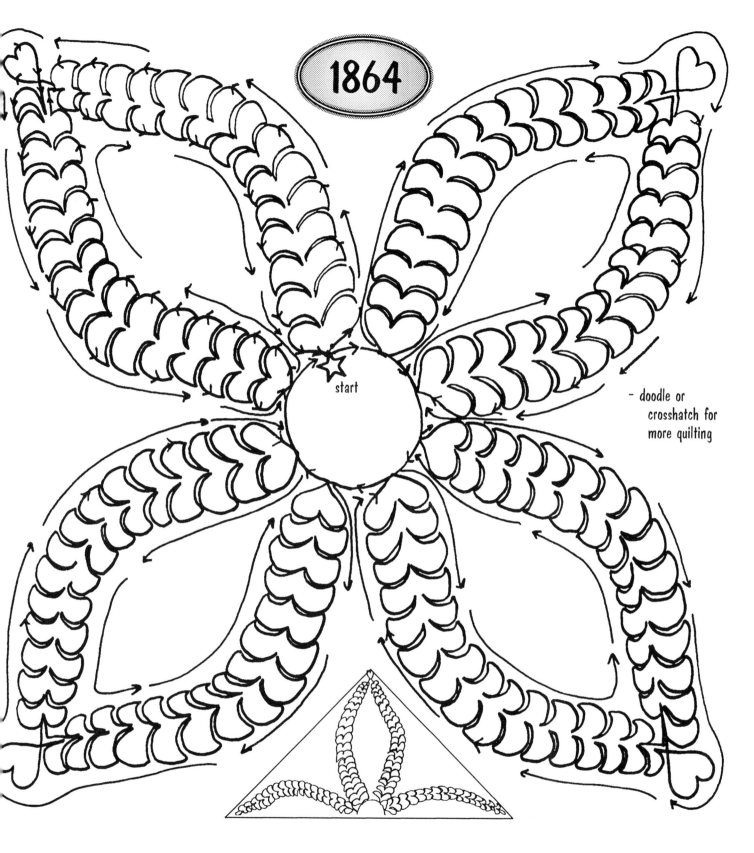

1864

start

- doodle or crosshatch for more quilting

1-Use darning foot.
2-Quilt one frond at a time.
3-Quilt up one side of leaves.
4-Quilt heart then quilt down the outside leaves.
5-Start quilting up the inside left, then down the inside right.
6-Follow the inner circle to the next frond and repeat process.

- quilt a spine for each set of leaves before quilting
- think of the rounded parts as hearts

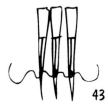

1-Use darning foot.
2-Quilt spine starting at the inside. Quilt leaves up the inside. Stitch across the intersection then stitch up the outside.
3-Continue alternating inside-outside until complete.
4-Repeat process on the opposite side.

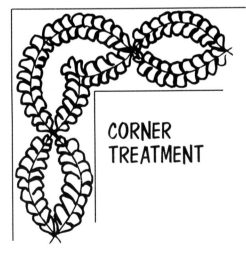

CORNER
TREATMENT

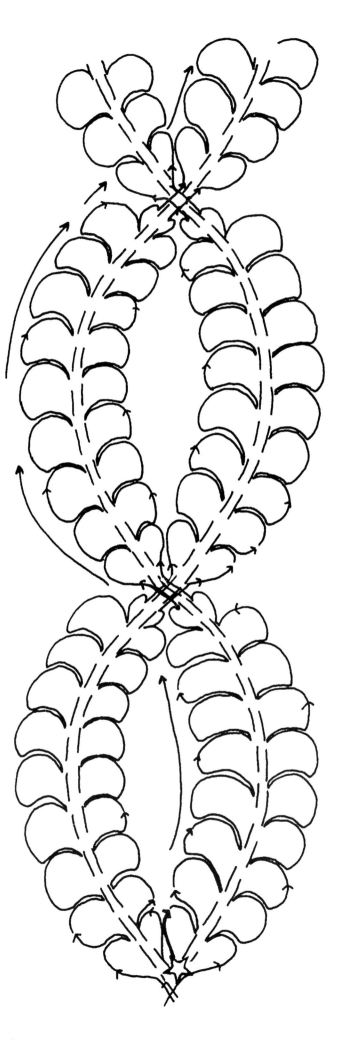

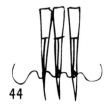

1-Use a darning foot.
2-Quilt inside design first in one
   continuous motion.
3-Reverse direction at the top and
   quilt outside design.
4-Repeat this design unit around
   borders or sashings.

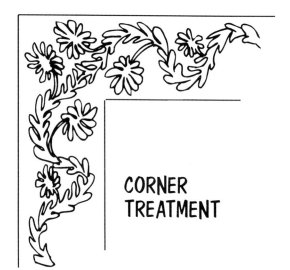

CORNER
TREATMENT

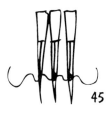

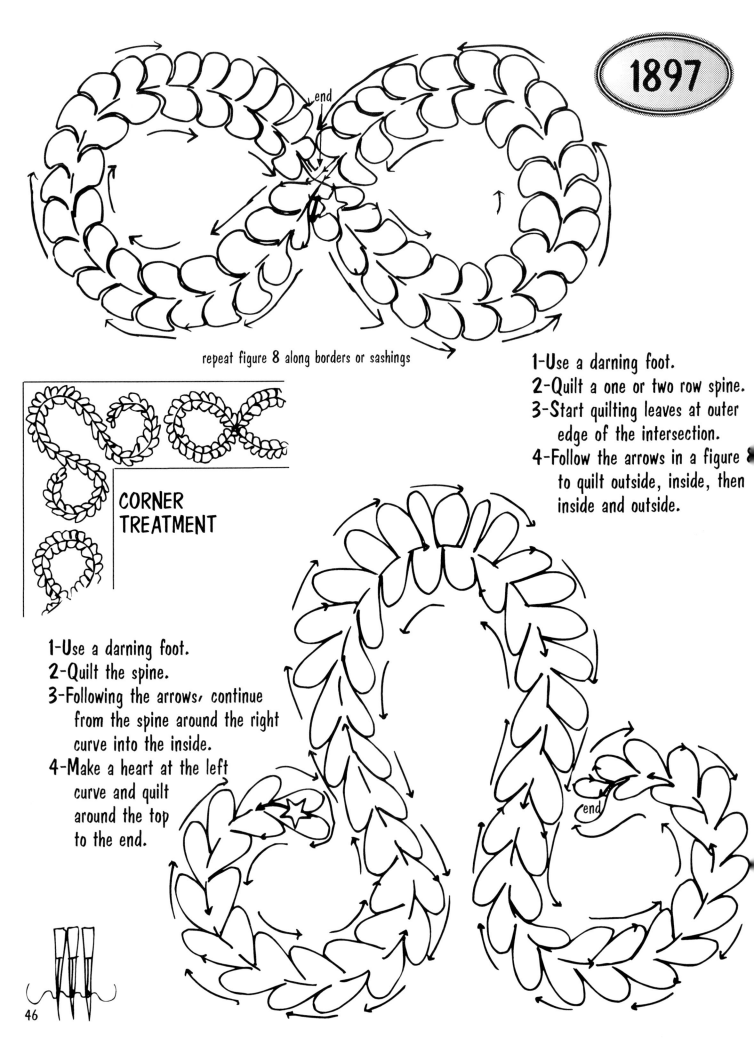

end

repeat figure 8 along borders or sashings

CORNER
TREATMENT

1-Use a darning foot.
2-Quilt a one or two row spine.
3-Start quilting leaves at outer
   edge of the intersection.
4-Follow the arrows in a figure 8
   to quilt outside, inside, then
   inside and outside.

1-Use a darning foot.
2-Quilt the spine.
3-Following the arrows, continue
   from the spine around the right
   curve into the inside.
4-Make a heart at the left
   curve and quilt
   around the top
   to the end.

end

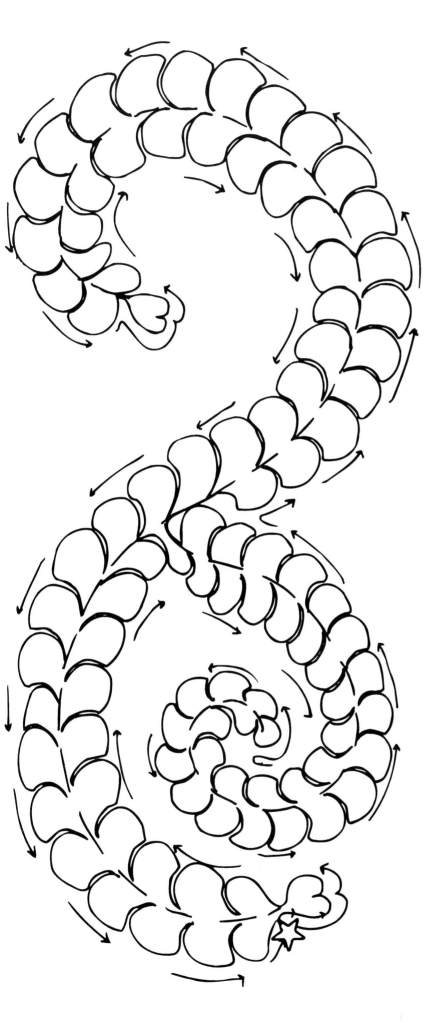

1-Use a darning foot.
2-Quilt a one or two row spine.
3-Begin quilting at star and
   follow arrows around the
   design.

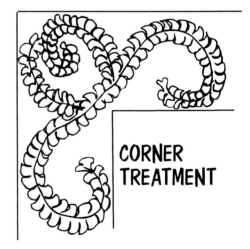

CORNER
TREATMENT

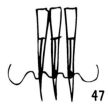

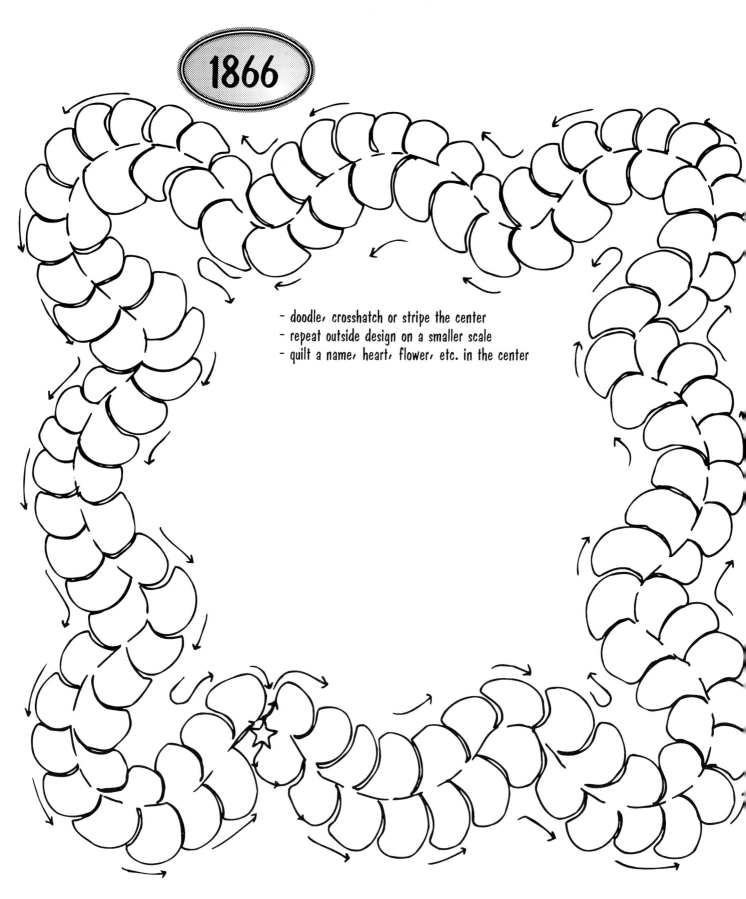

1866

- doodle, crosshatch or stripe the center
- repeat outside design on a smaller scale
- quilt a name, heart, flower, etc. in the center

1-Use darning foot.
2-Quilt a one or two row spine.
3-Begin at star and quilt inside leaves. Stitch to outside
   and quilt outside leaves.

Hearts
and Flowers

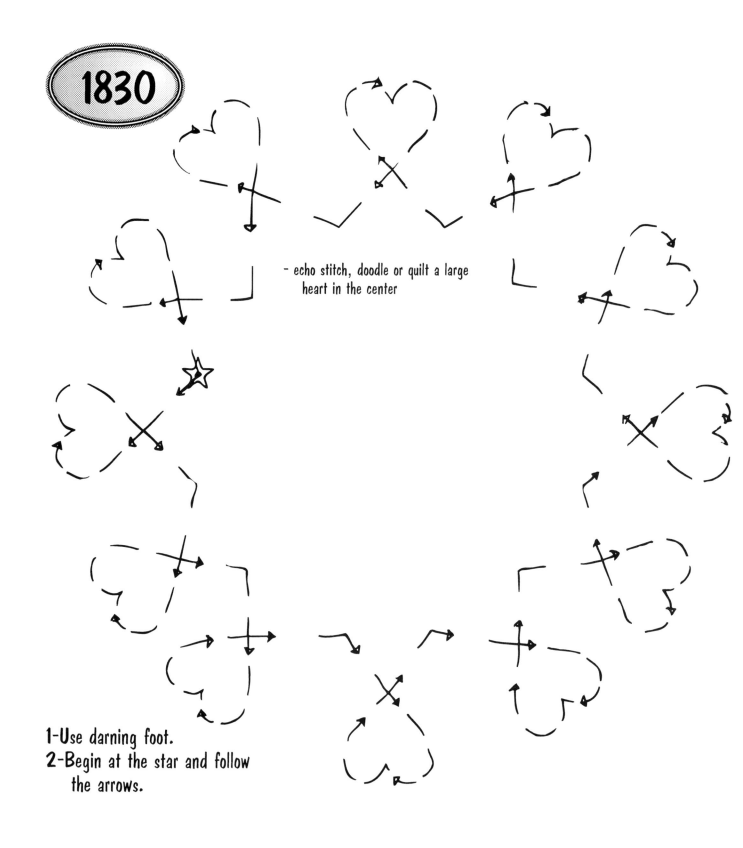

1830

– echo stitch, doodle or quilt a large heart in the center

1-Use darning foot.
2-Begin at the star and follow the arrows.

BORDER TREATMENT

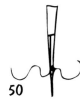

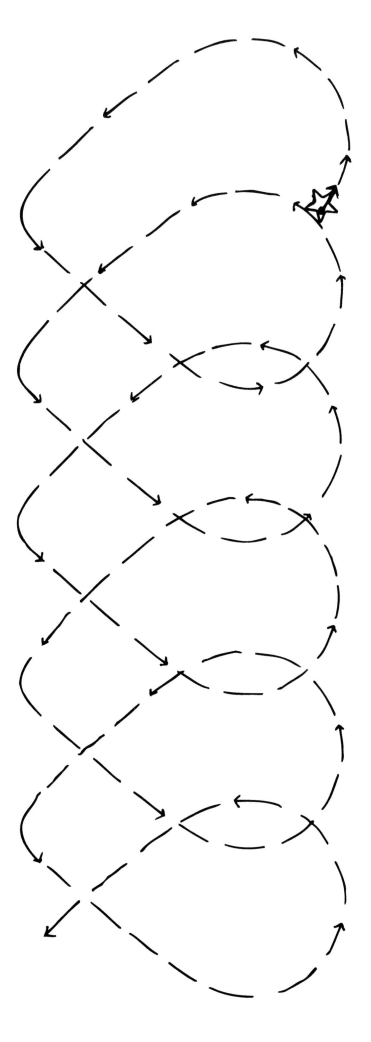

1-Use darning foot or walking foot.
2-Begin quilting at the star.
3-Follow the arrows loop-the-loop
  forming hearts.

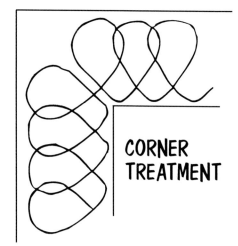

CORNER
TREATMENT

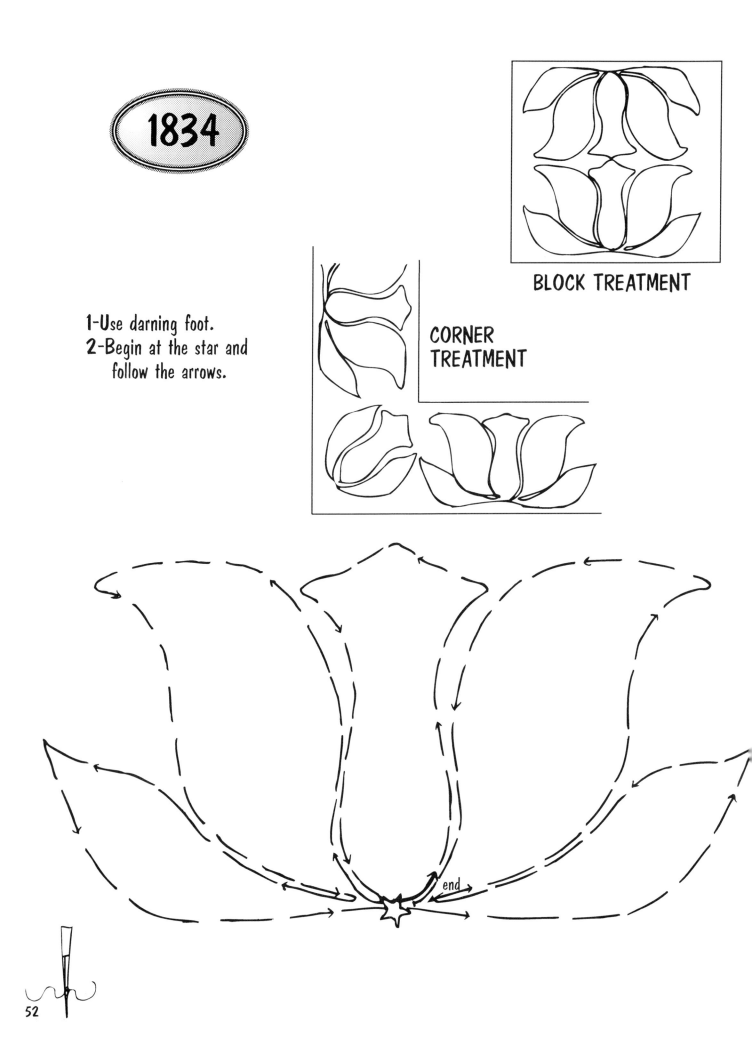

1834

1- Use darning foot.
2- Begin at the star and follow the arrows.

BLOCK TREATMENT

CORNER
TREATMENT

end

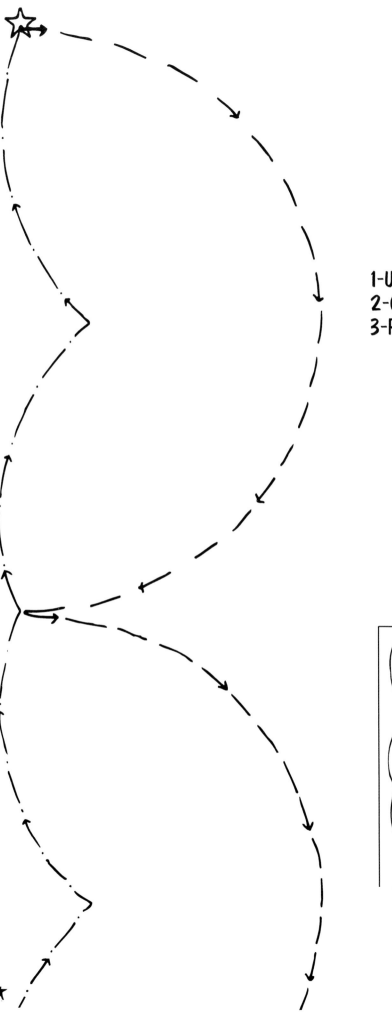

- echo quilt or place a flower or
leaf inside leaf shape

1-Use a darning foot or walking foot.
2-Quilt large curves following arrows.
3-Reverse direction and quilt small
   curves back to the beginning.

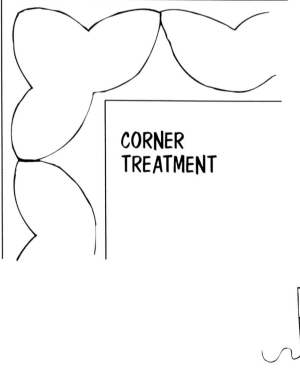

CORNER
TREATMENT

53

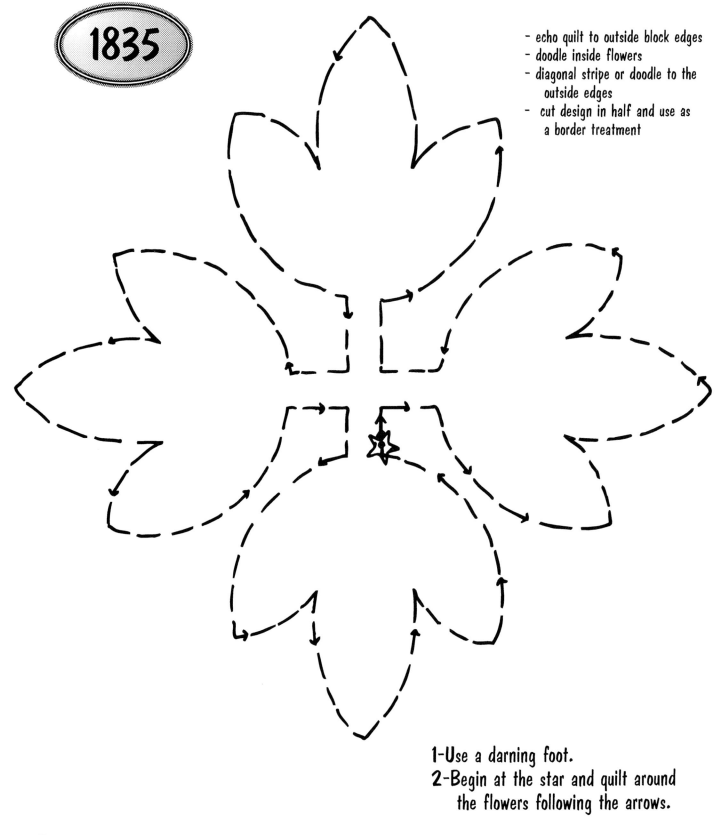

1835

- echo quilt to outside block edges
- doodle inside flowers
- diagonal stripe or doodle to the outside edges
- cut design in half and use as a border treatment

1-Use a darning foot.
2-Begin at the star and quilt around the flowers following the arrows.

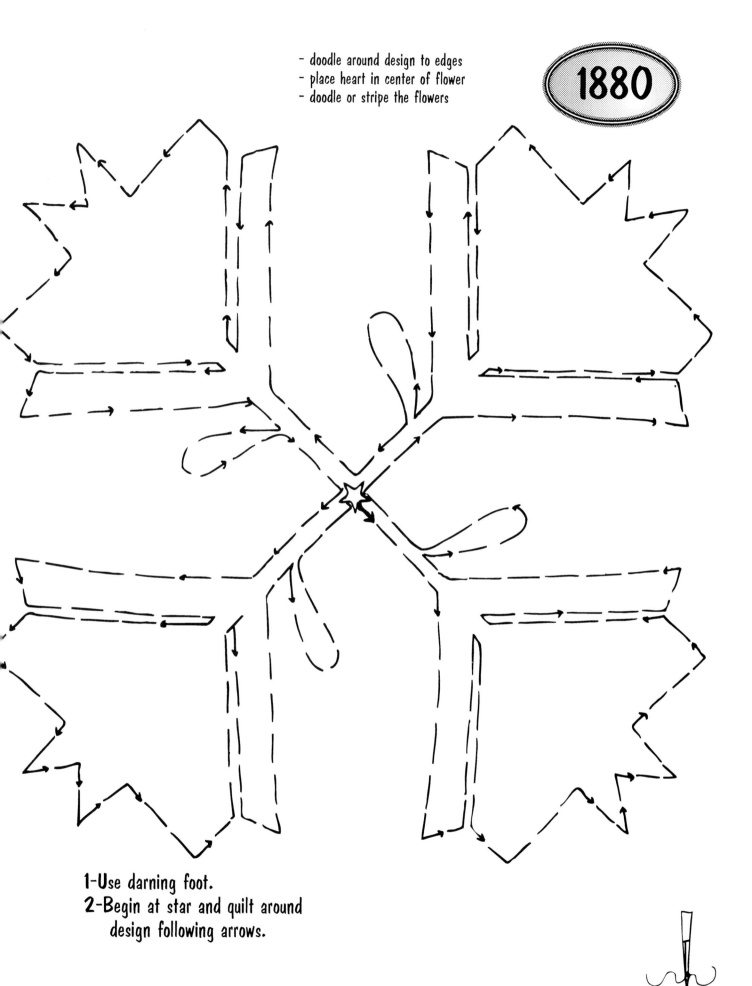

- doodle around design to edges
- place heart in center of flower
- doodle or stripe the flowers

1880

1-Use darning foot.
2-Begin at star and quilt around
  design following arrows.

1860

1-Use darning foot.
2-Follow arrows.
3-Repeat.

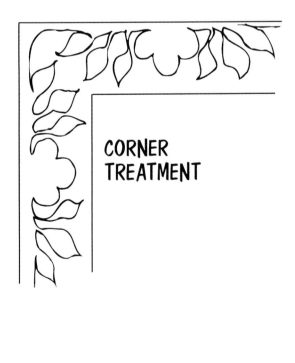

CORNER
TREATMENT

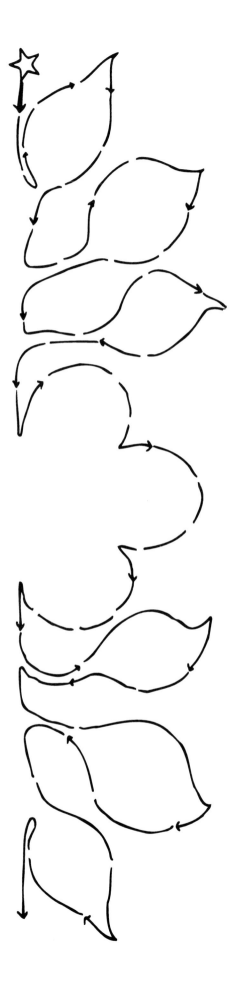

56

- echo quilt, diagonal stripe or doodle to block edges
- doodle inside flowers
- cut design in half and use as a border or
  corner treatment

1890

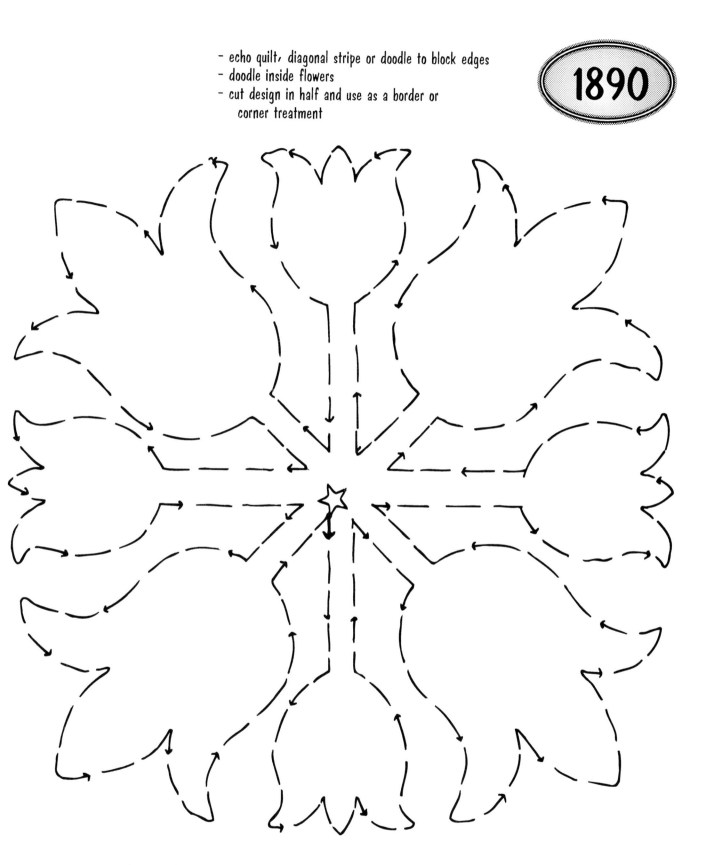

1-Use darning foot.
2-Begin at star and follow the arrows.

- echo quilt the center when using the
  block arrangement
- doodle the center of the hearts
- echo the center or outside of the hearts

CORNER TREATMENT

reduce original design 86% for this 8" block

1-Use darning foot.
2-Quilt inner petal, outer petal, heart,
    outer petal, inner petal.
3-Repeat design.

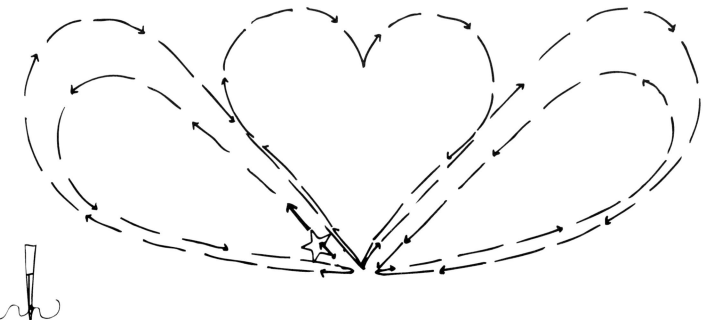

- doodle in the center or outside to the edges
- echo stitch to outer edges
- echo center design

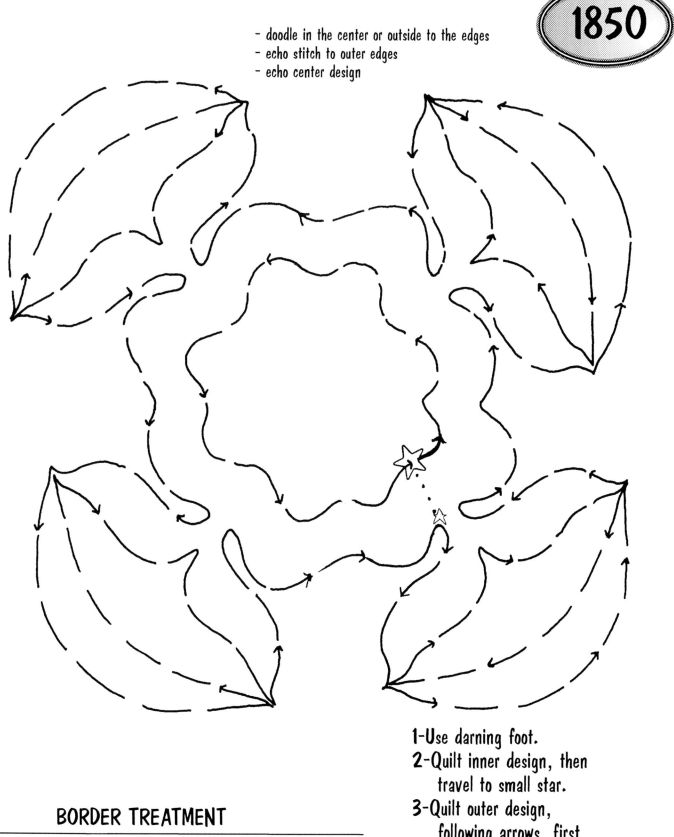

1-Use darning foot.
2-Quilt inner design, then travel to small star.
3-Quilt outer design, following arrows, first around arch of the flower then the leaves.

BORDER TREATMENT

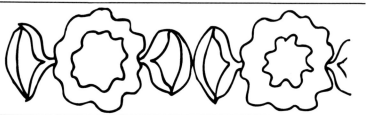

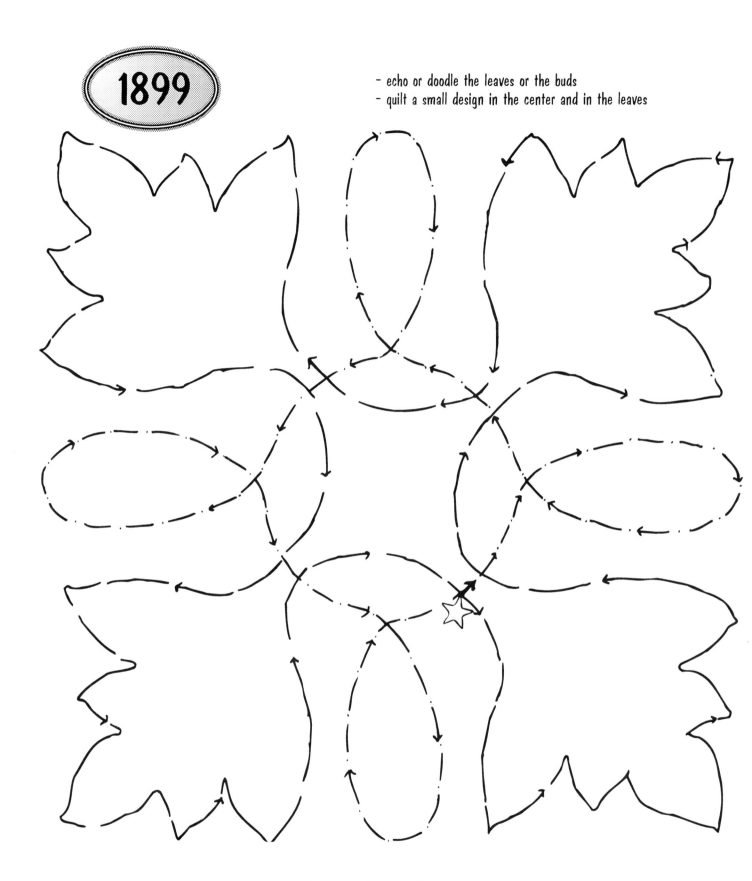

1899

- echo or doodle the leaves or the buds
- quilt a small design in the center and in the leaves

1-Use a darning foot.
2-Quilting is done in two steps. Begin at the star and quilt the loop-the-loops.
3-From the end of previous quilting, stitch the leaves and follow the arrows, ending where you began.

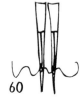

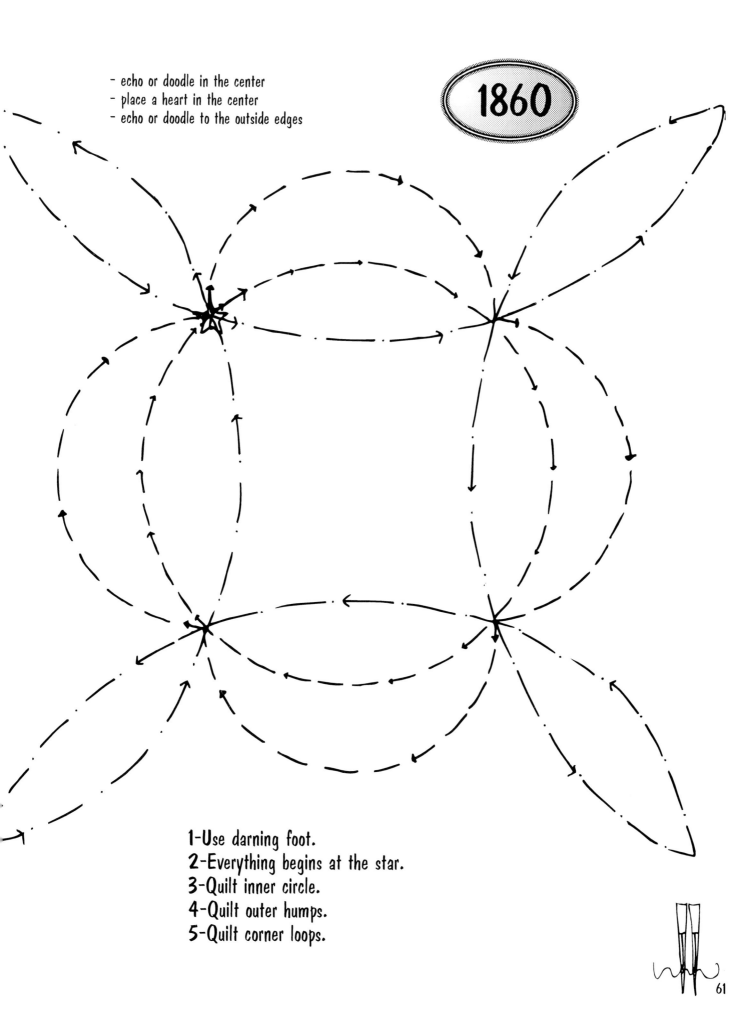

- echo or doodle in the center
- place a heart in the center
- echo or doodle to the outside edges

1860

1-Use darning foot.
2-Everything begins at the star.
3-Quilt inner circle.
4-Quilt outer humps.
5-Quilt corner loops.

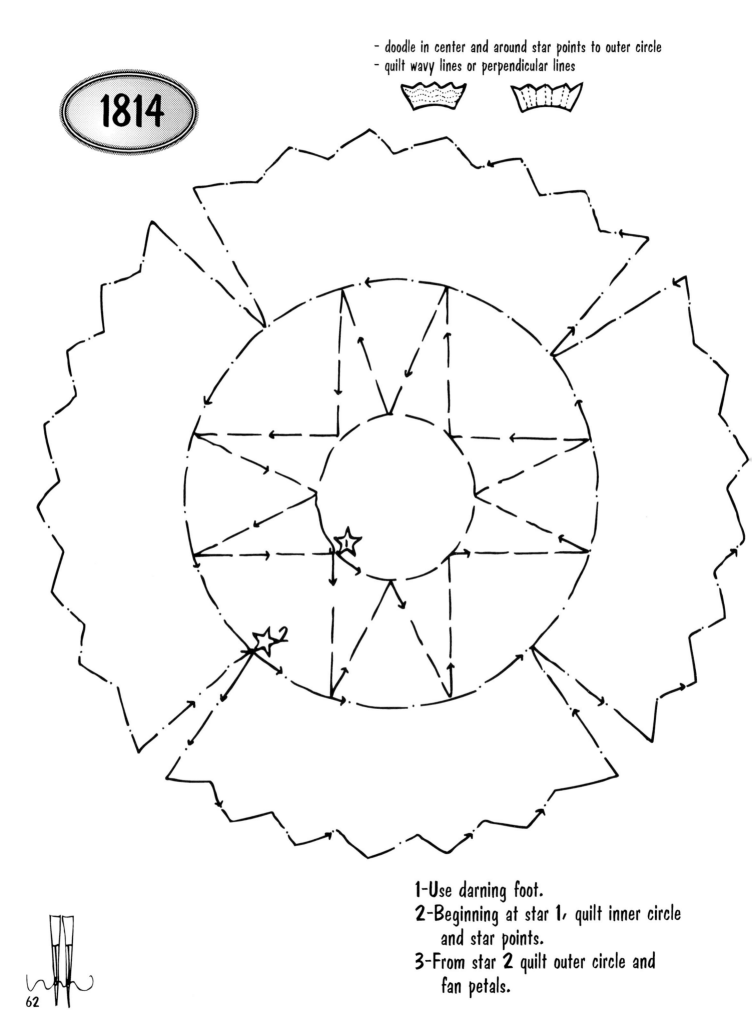

1814

- doodle in center and around star points to outer circle
- quilt wavy lines or perpendicular lines

1-Use darning foot.
2-Beginning at star **1**, quilt inner circle and star points.
3-From star **2** quilt outer circle and fan petals.

BLOCK TREATMENT

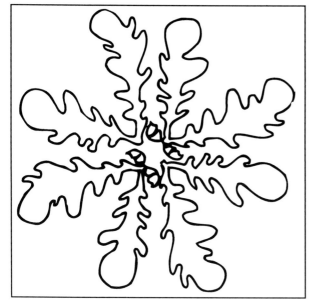

1-Use darning foot.
2-Begining at the star, quilt top side of acorn, around and back out to form the seat.
3-Quilt leaves.
4-Repeat acorn.

BORDER TREATMENT

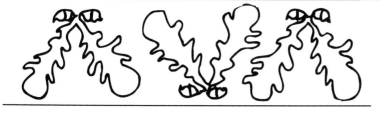

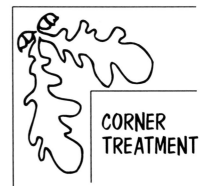

CORNER TREATMENT

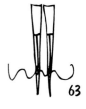

1854

- as your quilting improves you will be able to meander wherever you wish
- the leaves are meant to be irregular for a more natural appearance

1-Use darning foot.
2-Follow the arrows.
3-Repeat the design.

CORNER
TREATMENT

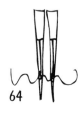

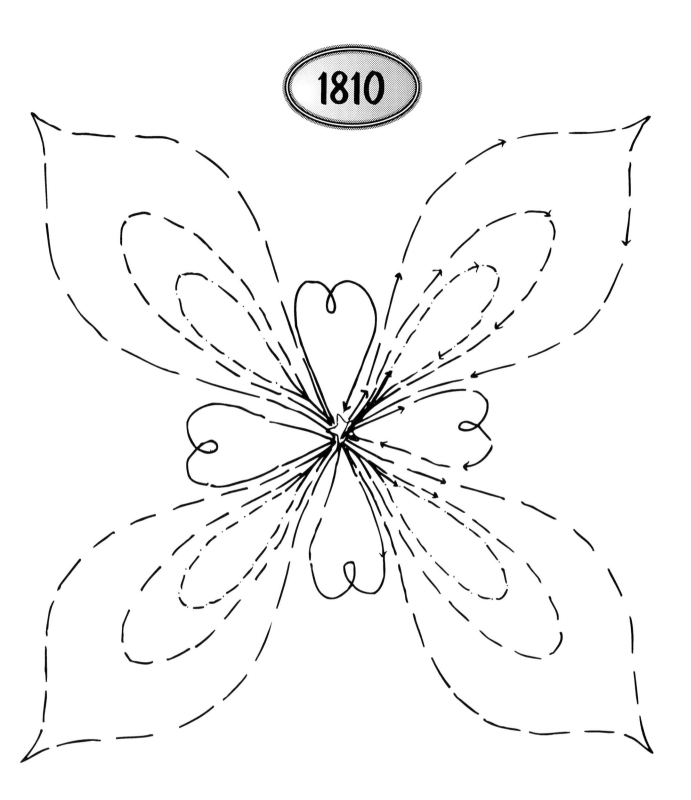

1810

1-Use darning foot.
2-Begin at the star.
3-Quilt the smallest leaf.
4-Quilt inner leaf back to the beginning point.
5-Quilt outer leaf back to the beginning point.
6-Pass through beginning point to base of adjoining heart
    and follow arrows.
7-Repeat for other leaves.

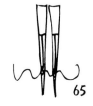

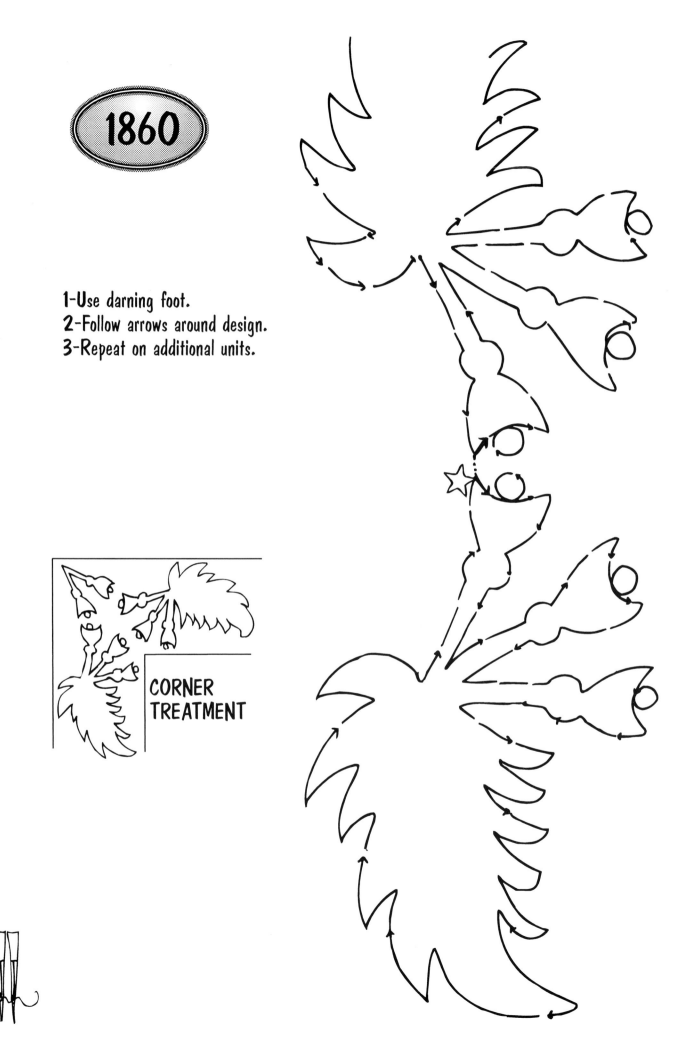

1860

1-Use darning foot.
2-Follow arrows around design.
3-Repeat on additional units.

CORNER
TREATMENT

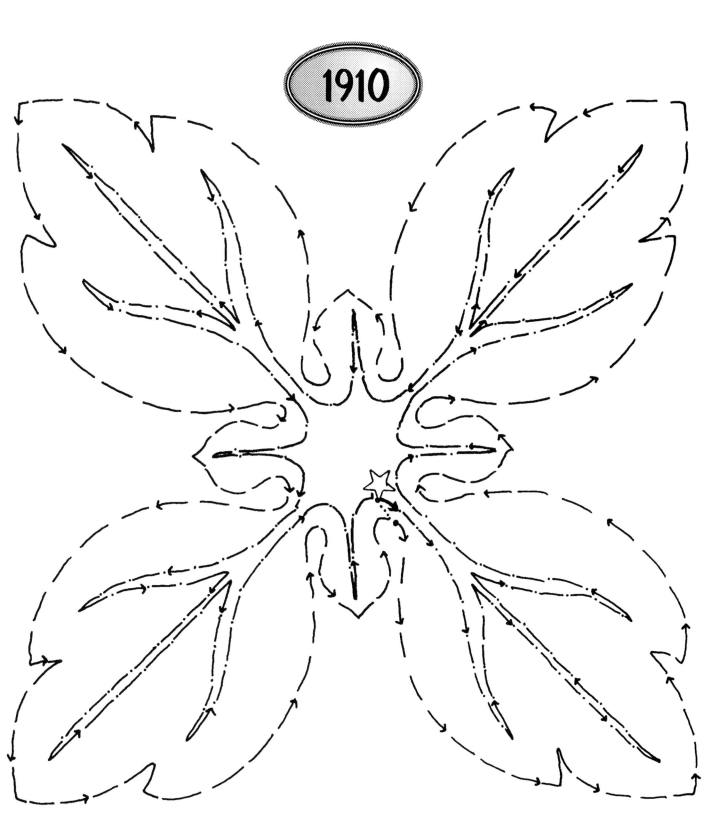

1910

1-Use darning foot.
2-Quilt inner veins first.
3-Travel to outside leaves and quilt.

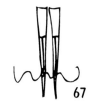

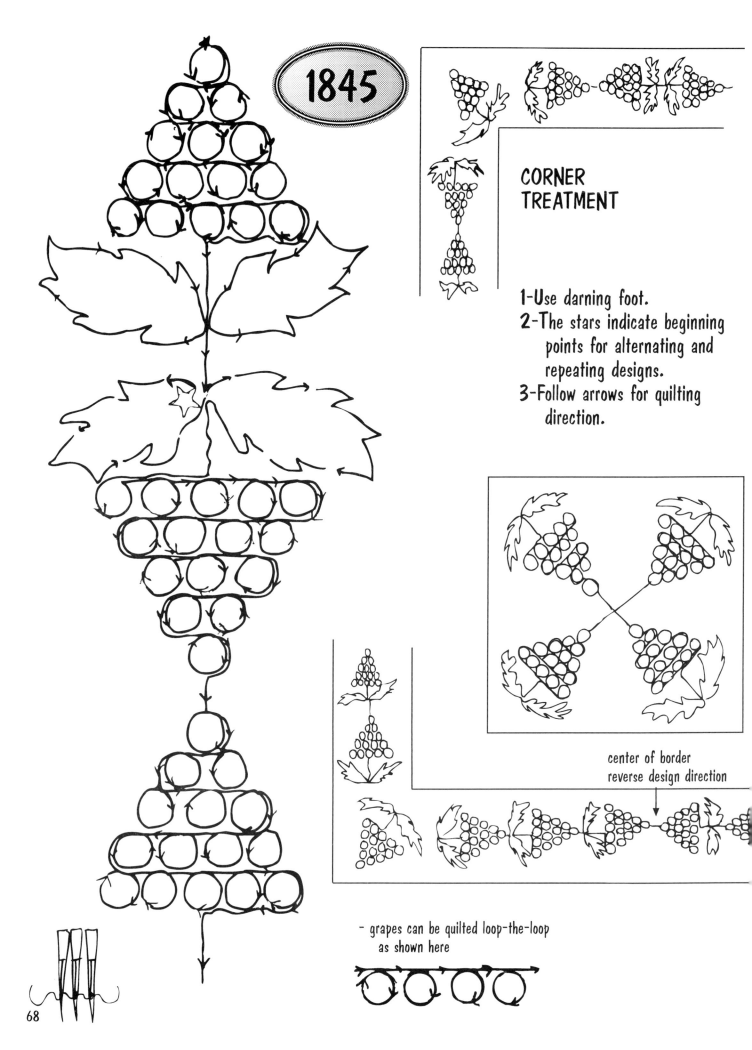

1845

CORNER
TREATMENT

1-Use darning foot.
2-The stars indicate beginning
   points for alternating and
   repeating designs.
3-Follow arrows for quilting
   direction.

center of border
reverse design direction

- grapes can be quilted loop-the-loop
  as shown here

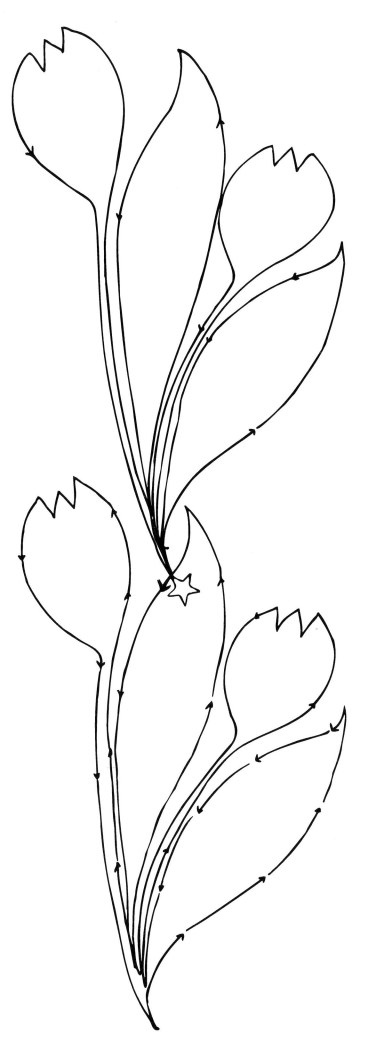

1929

1-Use darning foot.
2-Beginning at the star, quilt leaves, stems and flowers.
3-Follow arrows back to the beginning.
4-Start second grouping at the edge of the leaf. Follow arrows.
5-Repeat process, quilting in pairs for a border.

– begin quilting block in the center

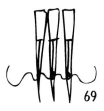

1850

- add as many buds as desired by replacing leaves with bud quilting
- make a continuous vine by omitting the top bud until reaching the end

1-Use darning foot.
2-Beginning at the star, follow arrows around leaves to the rose bud.
3-Quilt the spiral to the center, then quilt to the outer edge of the spiral and complete the bud.
4-Continue on each side back to the beginning.

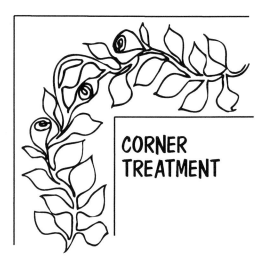

CORNER TREATMENT

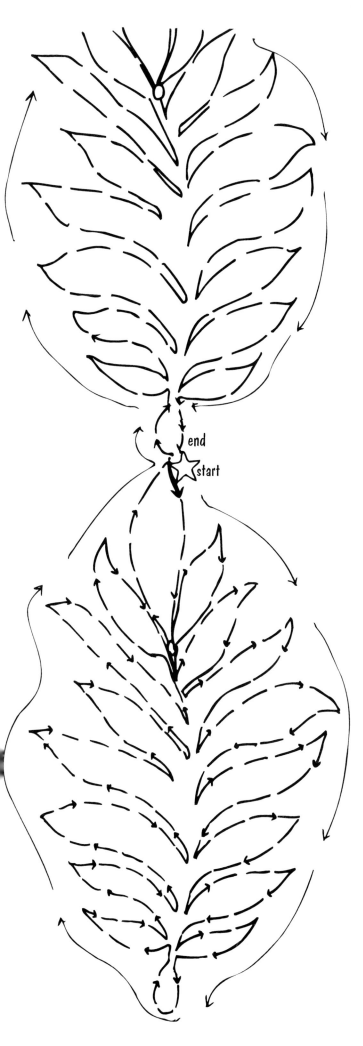

end

start

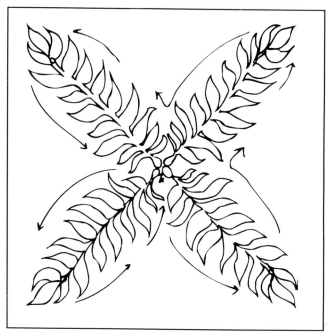

1-Use darning foot.
2-Follow arrows.
3-Repeat motif, end-to-end or
    flower-to-flower.

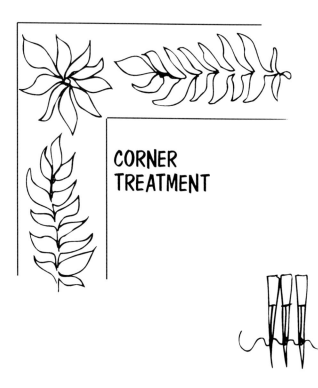

CORNER
TREATMENT

1810

1-Use darning foot.
2-Starting in the center, quilt a figure 8 vertically, then horizontally.
3-Still at center, quilt two pointed leaves in each quarter. Travel from one quadrant to the next through the center.
4-Quilt outer star petals.

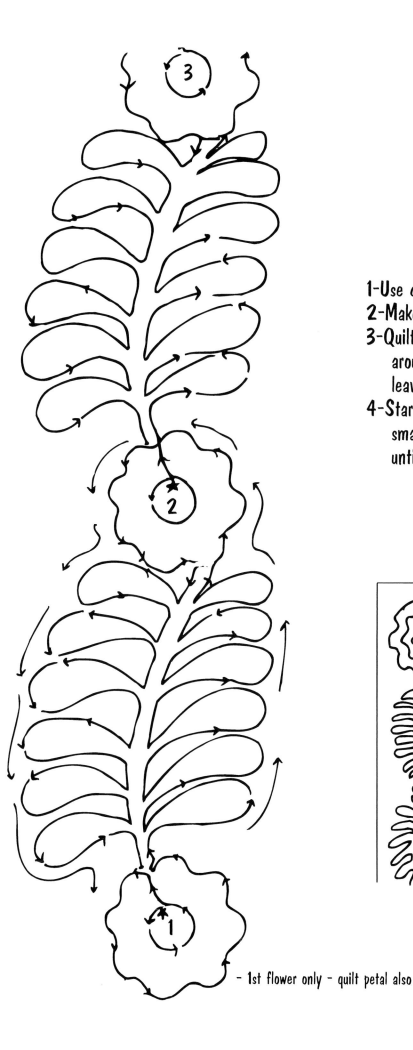

1-Use darning foot.
2-Make first flower as shown.
3-Quilt right side leaves, then quilt
   around flower and down left side
   leaves to the end.
4-Start second unit by quilting the
   small circle, then the leaves. Repeat
   until border is complete.

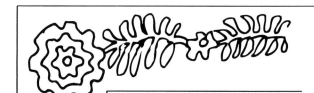

CORNER
TREATMENT

- 1st flower only - quilt petal also

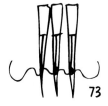

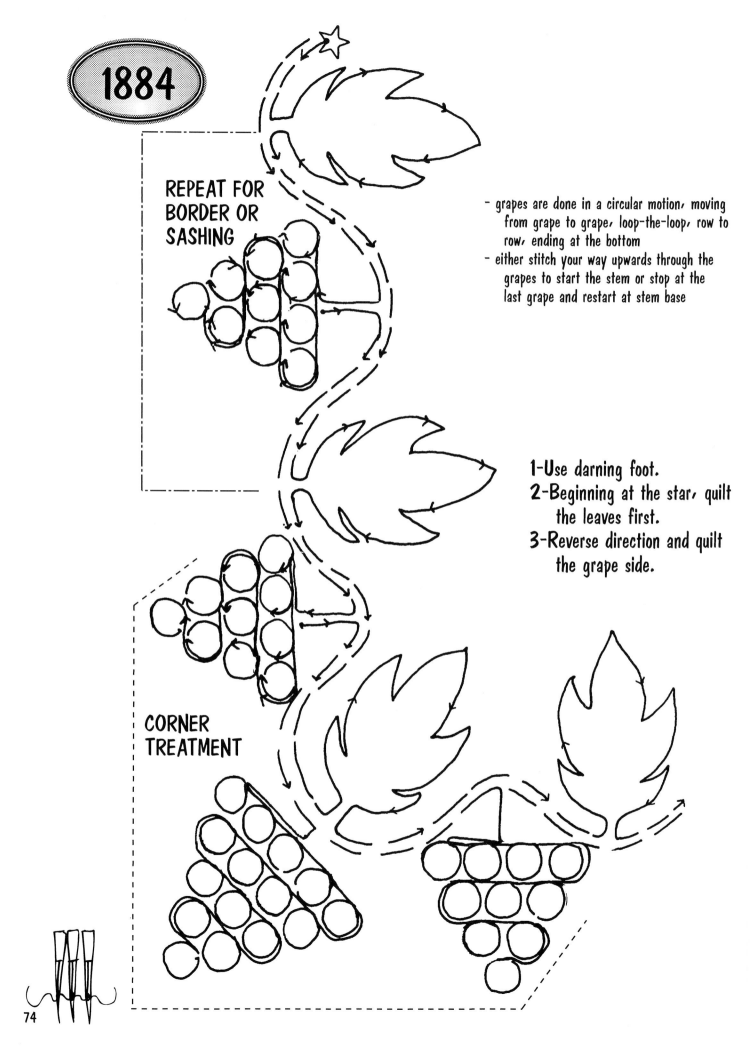

1884

REPEAT FOR
BORDER OR
SASHING

- grapes are done in a circular motion, moving
  from grape to grape, loop-the-loop, row to
  row, ending at the bottom
- either stitch your way upwards through the
  grapes to start the stem or stop at the
  last grape and restart at stem base

1-Use darning foot.
2-Beginning at the star, quilt
   the leaves first.
3-Reverse direction and quilt
   the grape side.

CORNER
TREATMENT

74

Seasonal
and Swags

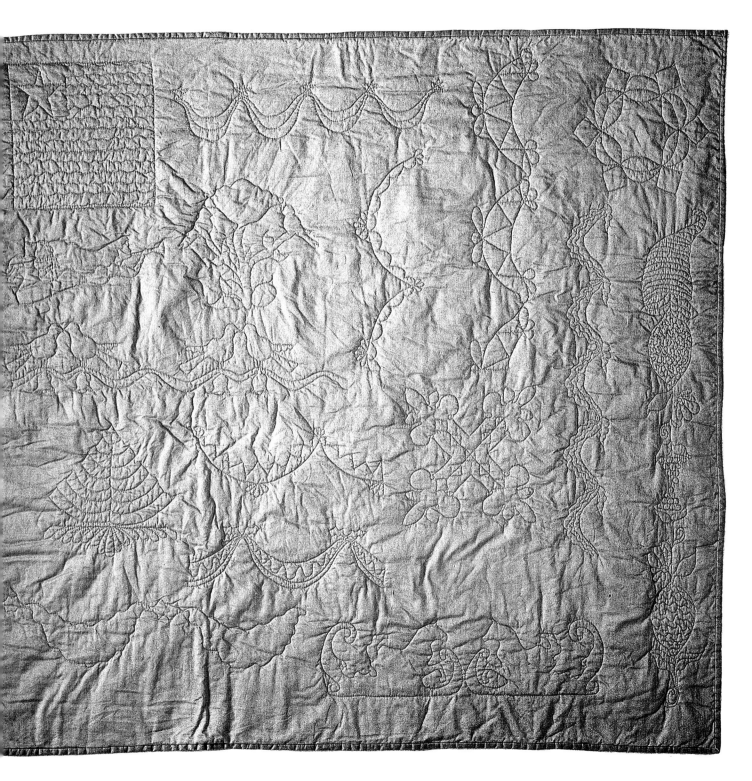

1872

1-Use darning foot.
2-Begin quilting in the seam line.
3-Continue quilting rows following the arrows.
4-Upon completion of final row, stitch-in-the-ditch back to the beginning.

reduce 50% for border

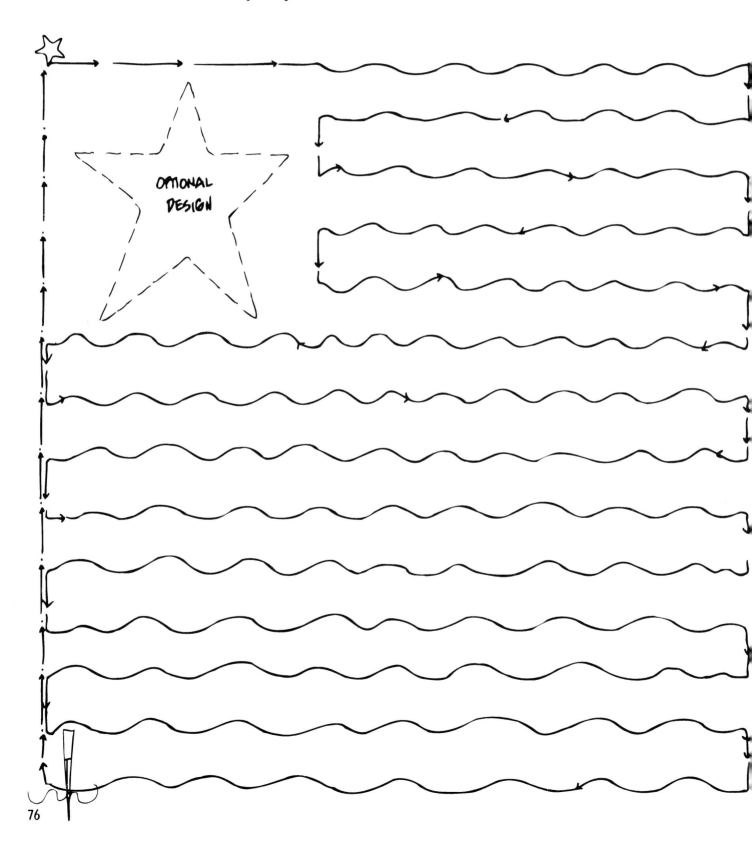

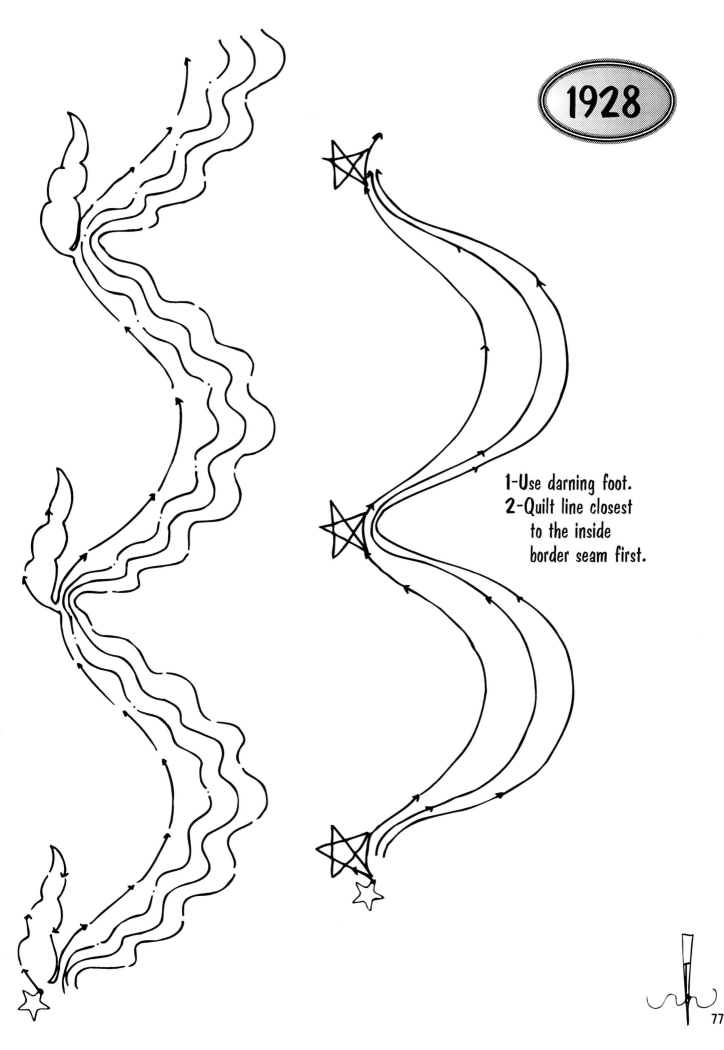

1-Use darning foot.
2-Quilt line closest
   to the inside
   border seam first.

1820

— curve may go in or out

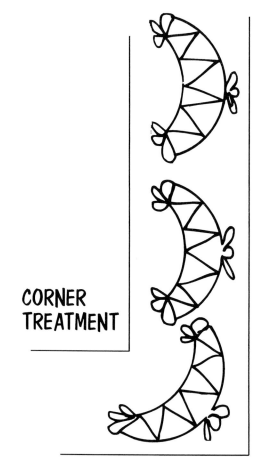

CORNER
TREATMENT

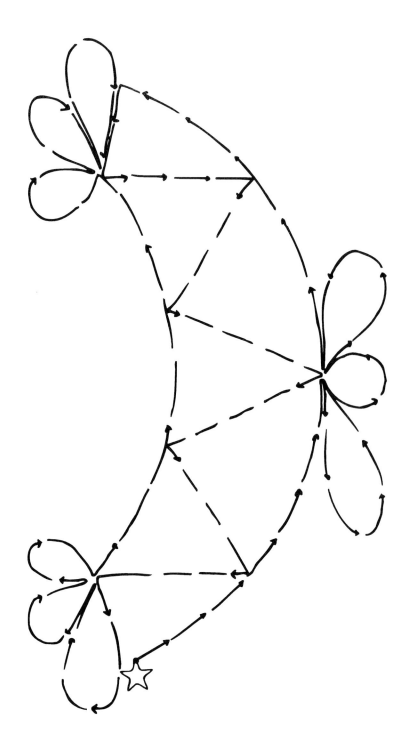

1-Use darning foot.
2-Begin quilting outer curve including flower.
3-Quilt zig-zag.
4-Quilt lower flower.
5-Quilt inner curve, ending with opposite flower.
6-Repeat.

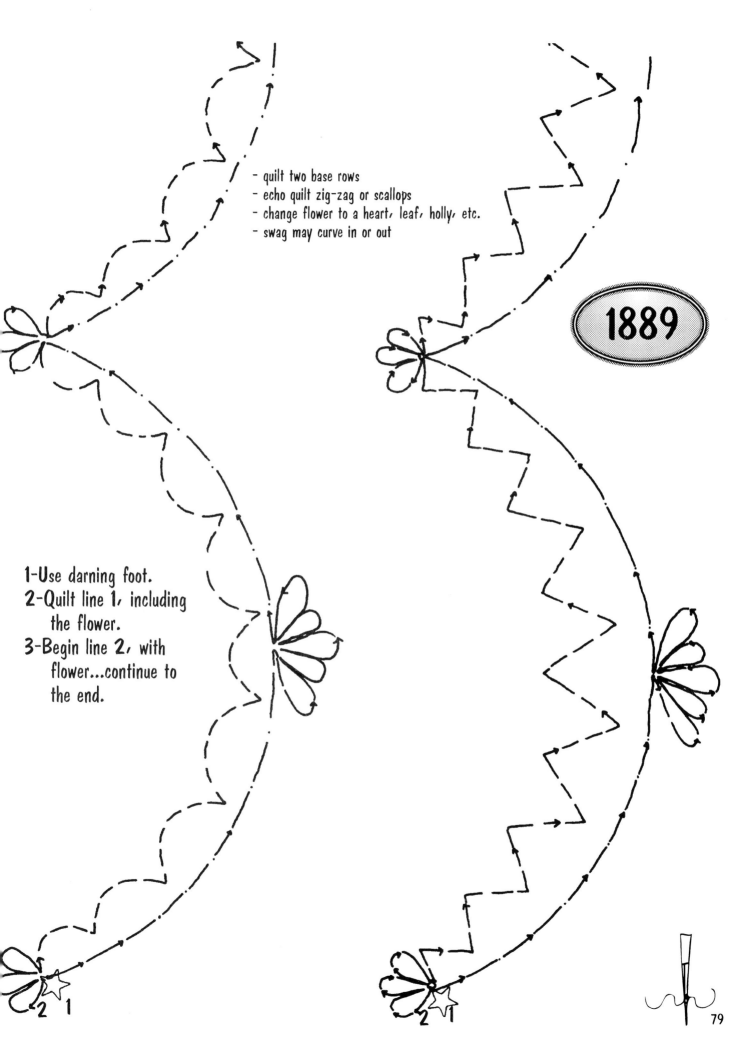

- quilt two base rows
- echo quilt zig-zag or scallops
- change flower to a heart, leaf, holly, etc.
- swag may curve in or out

1889

1-Use darning foot.
2-Quilt line 1, including
   the flower.
3-Begin line 2, with
   flower...continue to
   the end.

1864

- echo quilt inside the swags
- swags may curve in or out
- doodle around the swag

1–Use darning foot or
    walking foot.
2–Quilt inside curve first.
    Holly leaf will join swags
    together.
3–Quilt outside curve, completing
    holly leaf in the process.

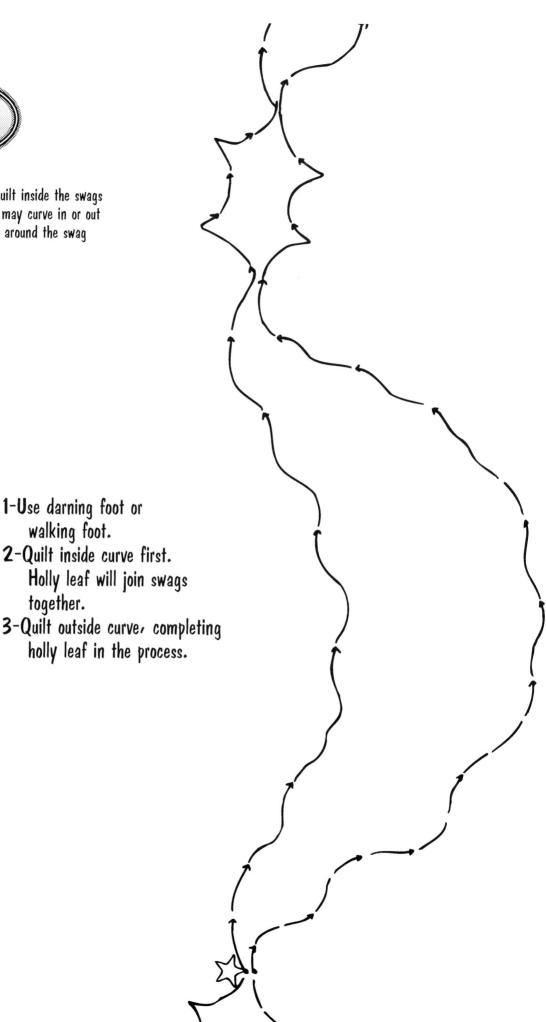

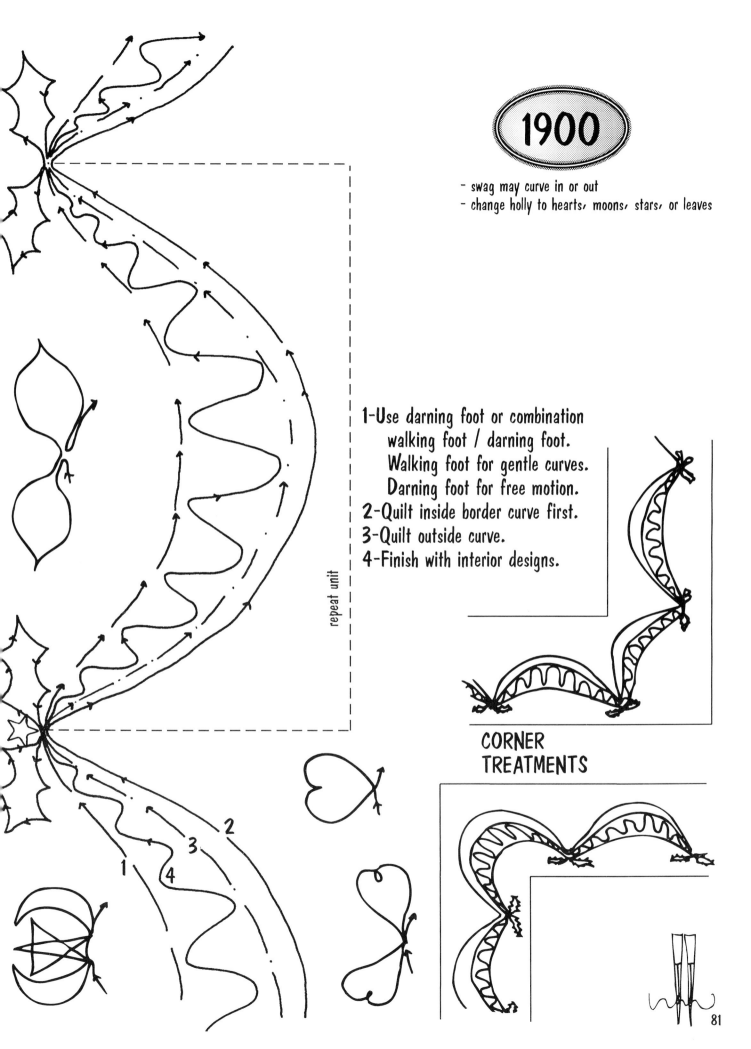

1900

- swag may curve in or out
- change holly to hearts, moons, stars, or leaves

repeat unit

1-Use darning foot or combination
    walking foot / darning foot.
    Walking foot for gentle curves.
    Darning foot for free motion.
2-Quilt inside border curve first.
3-Quilt outside curve.
4-Finish with interior designs.

CORNER
TREATMENTS

81

1840

- quilt seasonal designs in the center
  or replace diamonds with hearts,
  flowers, holly, leaves, apples.....
- doodle or crosshatch center

1-Use darning foot.
2-Begin quilting at star.
3-Quilt circle first.
4-Quilt inner loops.
5-Quilt diamonds and outer
  loops following arrows.

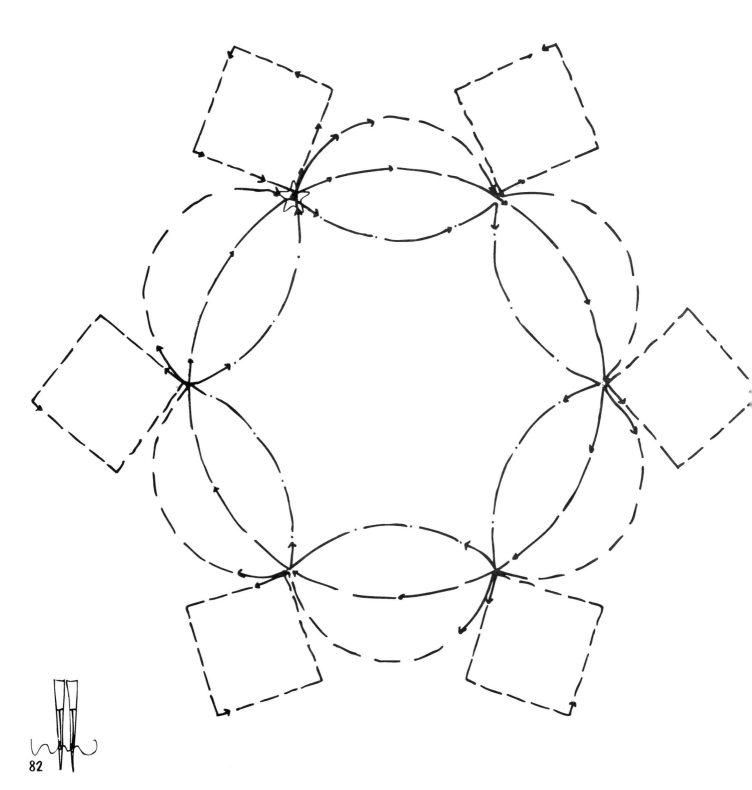

- quilt hearts, flowers or stars in the blank spaces between the designs

1875

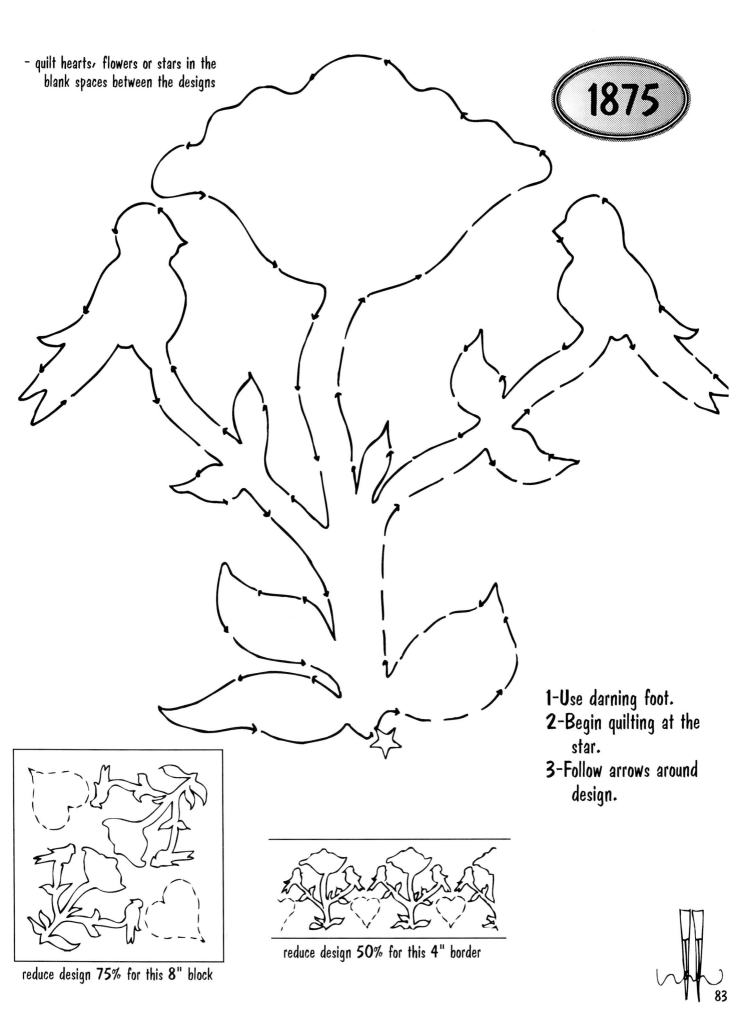

1-Use darning foot.
2-Begin quilting at the star.
3-Follow arrows around design.

reduce design 75% for this 8" block

reduce design 50% for this 4" border

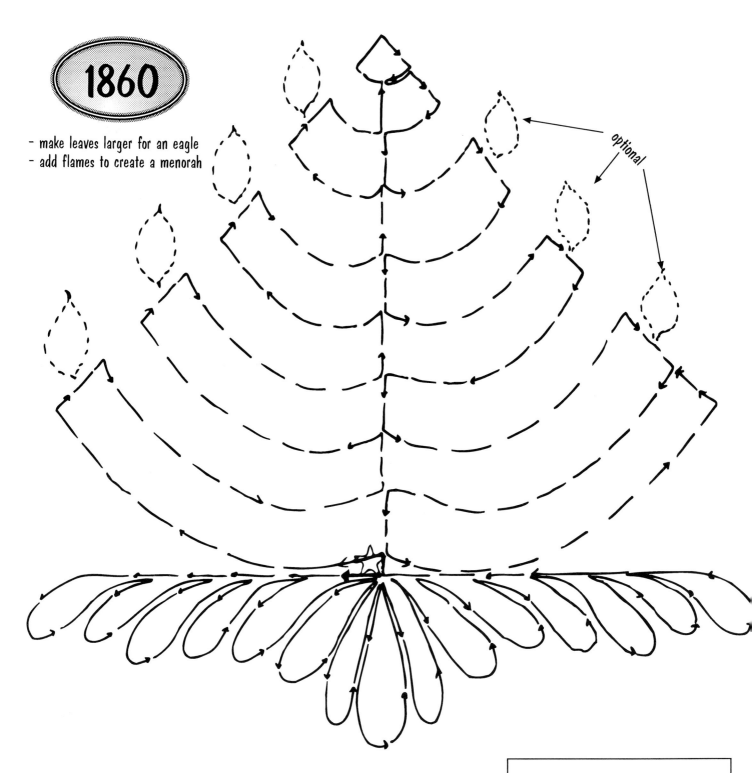

1860

- make leaves larger for an eagle
- add flames to create a menorah

optional

1-Use darning foot.
2-Beginning at the star quilt leaves first.
3-Quilt up left side of design.
4-At the top back-stitch to the edge of the first curve.
5-Quilt following arrows to the end.

1860

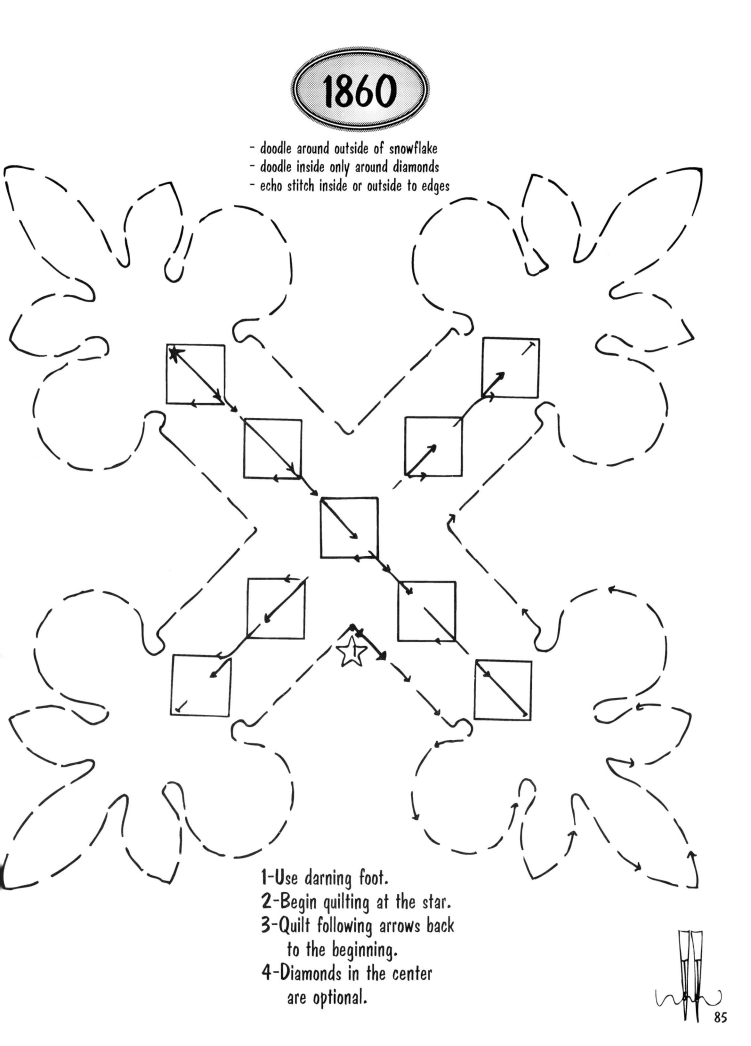

- doodle around outside of snowflake
- doodle inside only around diamonds
- echo stitch inside or outside to edges

1-Use darning foot.
2-Begin quilting at the star.
3-Quilt following arrows back
   to the beginning.
4-Diamonds in the center
   are optional.

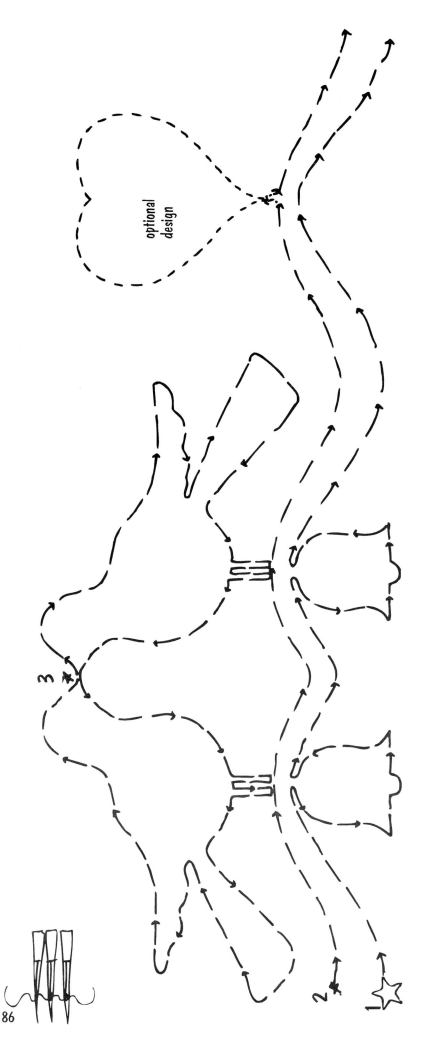

optional design

3

- other objects may be used for other seasons
- great for a wedding gift

1-Use darning foot.
2-Quilt in three steps. Begin with the bell curve, followed by the echo curve. Quilt the birds. Curves will become an anchor for the bird design.

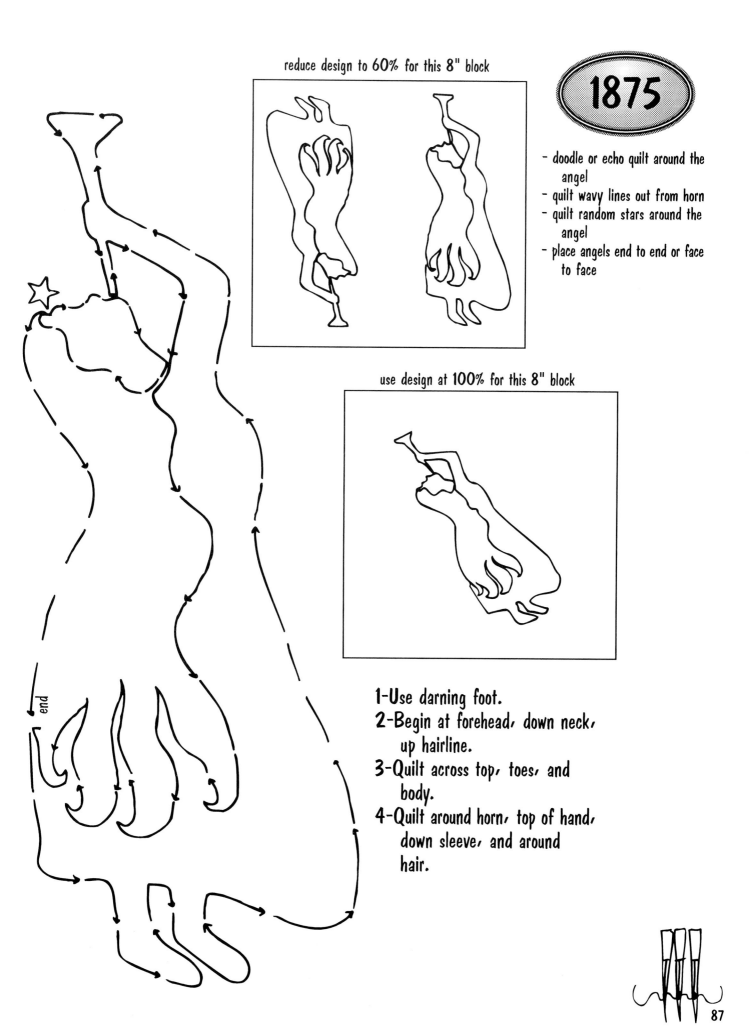

reduce design to 60% for this 8" block

1875

- doodle or echo quilt around the angel
- quilt wavy lines out from horn
- quilt random stars around the angel
- place angels end to end or face to face

use design at 100% for this 8" block

end

1-Use darning foot.
2-Begin at forehead, down neck, up hairline.
3-Quilt across top, toes, and body.
4-Quilt around horn, top of hand, down sleeve, and around hair.

1860

- fill in top of block with echo, doodle, stars, or snowflakes

reduce design **2%** for this **8"** block

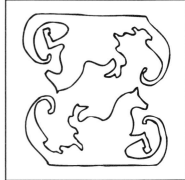

1-Use darning foot.
2-Begin quilting at star.
3-Quilt following arrows back
   to the beginning.

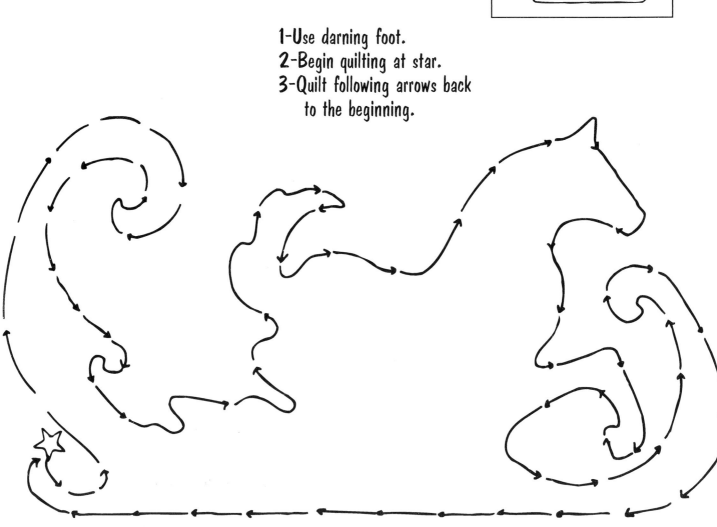

BORDER TREATMENT

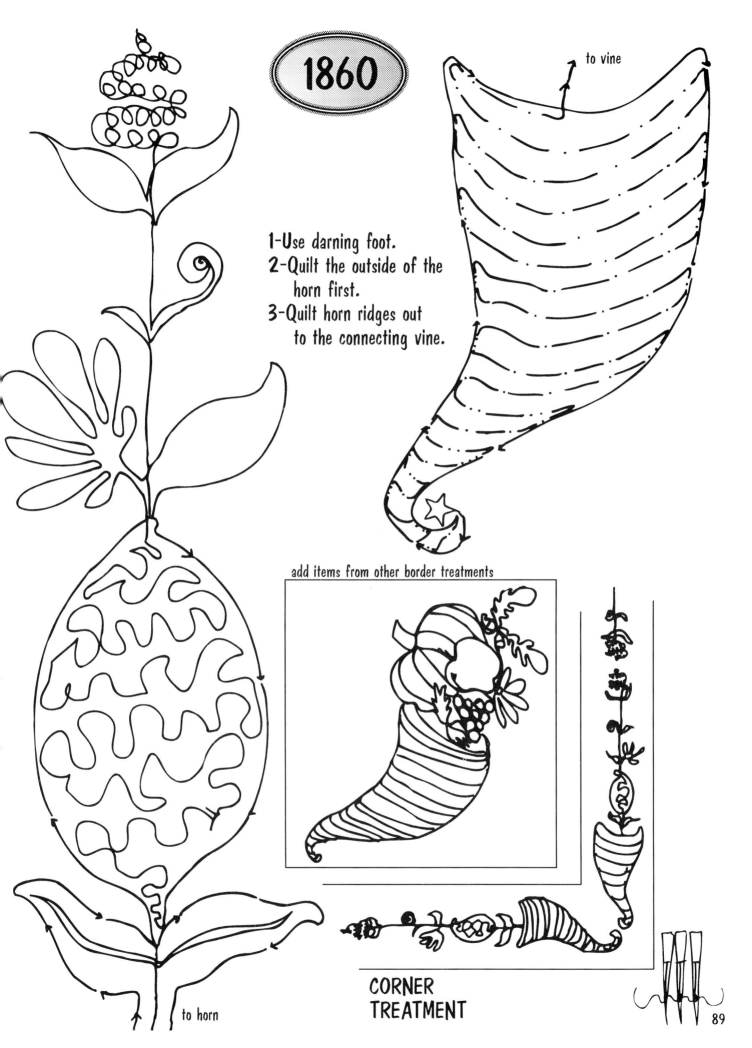

1860

to vine

1-Use darning foot.
2-Quilt the outside of the
   horn first.
3-Quilt horn ridges out
   to the connecting vine.

add items from other border treatments

CORNER
TREATMENT

to horn

1860

- use as corner treatments for
  vines, swags, feathers, or ferns
- repeat a design throughout border

1-Use darning foot.
2-Start at star and follow the arrows.

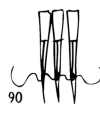

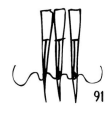

Other books by ANIMAS QUILTS PUBLISHING

WEAVER FEVER by Jackie Robinson $ 6.50
    Bargello type quilts in a woven design. Easy.

QUADCENTRICS by Jackie Robinson $ 7.00
    Designs which travel over and under each other.

TESSELLATIONS by Jackie Robinson $ 12.00
    Geometric shapes forming a repeating pattern.
    Inspired by M.C. Escher.

ON THE DOUBLE by Suzan Drury $ 14.00
    Two-for-one quilts cut from one basic strip set.

DINING DAZZLE by Jackie Robinson $ 16.00
    A collection of 20 placemats and 4 table runners.

REFLECTIONS by Melinda Malone $ 13.00
    Positive-negative designs in great quilts.

SIMPLY LANDSCAPES by Judy Sisneros $ 14.00
    Turn your favorite scene into a quilt with ease.

APPLIQUE, THE EASY WAY $ 20.00
    by Kathryn Kuhn and Timmie Stewart
    No basting or pressing with this easy method.

TAKE 2 by Joanna Myrick $ 14.00
    Eleven two-color quilts with complete directions.

STARBOUND by Susan Dillinger $ 8.00
    Coordinated treeskirts, stockings, table runners, etc.

CHILDREN'S ZOO by Barbara Morgan $ 18.00
    A safari of animals in quilts and accessories.

TERRIFIC TRIANGLES by Shelly Burge $ 18.00
    Slick tricks for scrappy half-square triangles.

QUILTS in the tradition of FRANK LLOYD WRIGHT $ 19.00
    by Jackie Robinson
    Eighteen designs based on Wright's art glass windows.

SENSATIONAL STARS by Gail Garber $ 15.00
    Create spectacular star quilts.

PERENNIAL PATCHWORK by Jackie Robinson $ 11.00
    A garden of flower blocks in eight different "sets".

STAR GAZING by Jackie Robinson $ 12.00
    Ohio stars in several variations.

CHAINS OF LOVE by Jackie Robinson $ 10.00
    Double and Triple Irish Chain quilts.

BINDING MITER TOOL $ 4.00
    Make mitered corners on quilt bindings
    easy and perfect every time.

PLEASE ADD POSTAGE:

$ 1.75 FOR 1 ITEM
$ 2.50 FOR 2 - 4 ITEMS
$ 3.50 FOR 5 - 9 ITEMS

THANK YOU!

Animas
Quilts
Publishing

600 Main Ave.
Durango, CO. 8130
(970) 247-2582